HISTORY'S MYSTERIES
FREAKY PHENOMENA

CURIOUS CLUES,
COLD CASES,
AND PUZZLES
FROM THE
PAST

KITSON JAZYNKA

NATIONAL
GEOGRAPHIC

WASHINGTON, D.C.

CONTENTS

DOOMED ARCTIC EXPEDITION

ABANDONED TOWER

We can't rewind the clock, but artifacts like this massive prehistoric image carved into the earth, and other clues like those from sunken ships or ruins of ancient structures, tell long-lost stories about the past.

INTRODUCTION

OUR UNIVERSE is full of mysteries. From intense black holes and an unknown planet that could be hiding in our very own solar system to dense, dark jungles and oceans deeper than Mount Everest is tall, every corner holds secrets waiting to be discovered. It's full of unimaginable places, unexplainable ancient objects, and surprises lurking right beneath the ground we walk on.

Experts are working hard to unearth ancient artifacts, search for never before seen stars, and dust off thousand-year-old bones. But for every new discovery they make, countless new mysteries are revealed. What are the secrets behind diamonds formed billions of years ago, toothy dinosaur-age predators as big as school buses, and a treacherous triangular trap in the Atlantic Ocean?

The answers to some of these far-out mysteries are lost to history. But for others, experts are hot on the trail. If you're ready to think like a great explorer (or a volcanologist, paleontologist, Egyptologist, geophysicist, or archaeologist), just turn the page!

Follow your curiosity on a fantastic journey with *National Geographic Kids History's Mysteries Freaky Phenomena*. Read the facts and learn all you can about what really happened way back when. Who knows ... maybe one day you'll be the archaeologist who finally discovers a long-lost city of gold in the Amazon—or the astronomer who discovers Planet Ten!

SECRETS OF THE
GREAT PYRAMID

BIZARRE BATTERIES

Millions of stars can be found
in groups called globular
clusters. Some stars are
billions of years old!

1
CREEPY
CREATURES

Nessie, is that you? This 3-D illustration of the monster in its natural habitat looks pretty convincing. But is there any real proof of this creature's existence?

MONSTERS ARE THE STUFF of legends and lore … right? Perhaps, but the tales are as old as time. Stories of mysterious beasts have been passed around for generations—often told while sitting around a campfire in the dark woods. But are these monster myths just time-honored traditions, or do some of them hold a shred of truth? Could Bigfoot really be the descendant of a surviving prehistoric ape and not just a figment of people's imagination? Is Mothman the winged spirit of revenge … or just an oversize bird? The debates rage on, and, according to some eyewitness accounts, so do the monsters. Believers and skeptics alike have worked for years to prove (or disprove) the existence of these unexplained creatures called cryptids. One thing's for sure: You'll never get to the bottom of this can of worms until you start investigating these eyewitness accounts of crazy creatures yourself.

YOU'LL HAVE TO **STICK** YOUR **NECK OUT** TO TRY TO FIGURE OUT THIS SUSPICIOUS SEA CREATURE.

LOOKING FOR NESSIE IN 1935

The first sighting of the
LOCH NESS MONSTER
was documented in
A.D. 565.

THE BACKGROUND

SCOTLAND'S HISTORY prickles with chilling legends. If you listen to the lore, this misty and mysterious land is full of supernatural beings, from deadly kelpies (sinister sea ponies) to werewolves to the famous lake beast called the Loch Ness Monster. This supersize swimmer is said to lurk in the canyons and dark caves at the bottom of the murky, peat-filled Loch Ness—a deep, cold lake in the middle of Scotland. At 788 feet (240 m) deep and 23 miles (36 km) long, this body of water holds the largest volume of freshwater in all of Great Britain. Even after plenty of underwater explorations, nobody really knows the whole story of what lives under the long lake's still, black surface. Sightings of the creature have confounded folks since the time of the Romans—long before Scotland was called Scotland. Dive deep to get to the bottom of this pond of freaky facts.

an artist's depiction of Nessie

ATLANTIC OCEAN

UNITED KINGDOM

EUROPE

AFRICA

Loch Ness

North Sea

UNITED KINGDOM

IRELAND

FRANCE

11

THE DETAILS

SCIENTISTS HAVE practically combed every inch of Loch Ness searching for its fabled monster. Tourists clamor to catch a glimpse, and some say they have seen or even photographed Nessie. The most common sightings involve people seeing what they think are scaly humps in the water or a head peeking above the waves. The creature is said to be gray with stubby legs, a small head, and a long neck. Modern-day fascination with notorious Nessie swelled in 1933 after a road was built along the lake, which allowed more people to check things out for themselves. The ancient lake beast is still trending, with new eyewitness accounts pouring in all the time. But what do we really know about this monster of a mystery?

THE CLUES
This freshwater monster is said to strike an eerie resemblance to a creature that lived during the time of the dinosaurs. Is it real or just local superstition gone viral? Here are three hints that help piece together this water-logged mystery:

EARLIEST IMAGES Prehistoric people carved images into stone (still standing today in the Loch Ness region) that look eerily like Nessie, with a long snout and flippers.

FAMOUS PHOTO In 1934, a doctor snapped a picture of a long-necked marine creature sticking its head out of the Loch Ness. Many believed the famous "surgeon's photo" proved the existence of Nessie. Others claimed it was a fake.

MASSIVE MONSTER A 1997 expedition sought to study the loch's biology and geology using sonar. But they also caught a flash of something that seemed to be the size of a whale moving through the Loch Ness.

THE RUINS OF URQUHART CASTLE OVERLOOK THE LOCH NESS.

USING SUBMARINES TO SEARCH THE LOCH NESS

THE THEORIES

SOME PEOPLE BELIEVE the mysterious animal is a surviving plesiosaur. That's right—they think that perhaps the great extinction that wiped out the dinosaurs some 80 million years ago missed a few. Plesiosaurs were giant creatures with long necks and paddle-like flippers that they used to propel themselves through water like penguins—a description that is eerily similar to those from eyewitnesses who claim to have spotted Nessie. And these accounts date way back to when a prehistoric tribe called the Picts—or painted people, as they once were called because they sported serious tattoos—lived in Scotland's highlands. The carvings they left behind on stones near Loch Ness look a lot like modern images of Nessie. They have experts wondering if plesiosaurs did indeed inhabit the area—and maybe still do.

But most experts say these plesiosaur theories sound a little fishy. One Scottish researcher, Steve Feltham, has spent 24 years investigating the legend. In 2015, he announced that he believed the Loch Ness monster is probably a much less mysterious kind of aquatic beast. He believes sightings of Nessie are actually sightings of an oversized Wels catfish. This whale of a fish can grow to be more than 13 feet (4 m) long and weigh about 900 pounds (408 kg). Wels catfish don't look much like Nessie, but Feltham thinks excited eyewitnesses confused one big swimmer for another.

Countless people claim to have seen Nessie in real life; some have even claimed to have captured the animal on film. The "evidence" was so convincing that, in the 1950s, four research expeditions used sonar to search underwater for clues. All they spotted was a bunch of water weeds. The strongest evidence came from the 1997 expedition when sonar detected a plus-size something paddling in the loch. The murky body of evidence has left many scientists and Nessie lovers alike swimming in doubt. But don't let the lack of facts dampen your enthusiasm for this ancient aquatic mystery. And if you decide to go looking, one bit of advice: Don't mess with the monster—you might be interfering with a highly endangered species.

NESSIE COULD BE RELATED TO PREHISTORIC PLESIOSAURS.

CHUPACABRA

THIS BEASTLY BLOODSUCKER IS ON THE PROWL.

THE BACKGROUND

WHEN GOATS AND CHICKENS turned up dead and drained of their blood in areas of Puerto Rico in the 1990s, rumors ran rampant about a menacing monster that was on the loose. The culprit was said to be a hairless vampire-like beast with fangs, red eyes, a darting forked tongue, quills running down its back—and a taste for livestock. Locals called it the Chupacabra. A few years later, many Texans also experienced an outbreak of mysterious livestock deaths. This time, people knew who to blame: the Chupacabra. The rumors spread, and today there have even been sightings of this morbid monster reported as far off as China. Do you think this is an urban legend run wild—or is there some terrifying truth to these accounts? What could this creepy, continent-hopping creature be?

UNITED STATES
PUERTO RICO

BAHAMAS

ATLANTIC OCEAN

HAITI DOMINICAN REPUBLIC

Puerto Rico

Caribbean Sea

"Chupacabra" translates roughly to "GOAT SUCKER" in SPANISH.

WHO—OR WHAT—WAS KILLING LIVESTOCK IN PUERTO RICO AND TEXAS?

THE DETAILS

HUNDREDS OF PEOPLE claim to have spotted the bloodthirsty baddie in the flesh, and in 2014, one couple even claimed to have captured it. But the "baby Chupacabra" they had trapped turned out to be nothing more than a large, hairless—and probably very freaked-out—raccoon. Read on to hear some clues about how this beast got its bad rap.

THE CLUES

Based on the large number of Chupacabra sightings over the years, we can assume one thing: It's not super shy. Bite into the details of these sickening sightings and see what you think.

 BALDING BEAST Hairlessness can be the result of mange, a disease that can cause a mammal's hair to fall out and its skin to scab and pucker, giving it a seriously sinister look.

SHADY SIGHTING In 1995, witnesses in Puerto Rico reported seeing a scary reptile-like creature with bulging red eyes and fanged teeth. The monster walked on two legs and stood about three feet (1 m) tall.

GRAVEYARD GHOUL In 2016, locals reported having seen a frightening fanged creature that matched descriptions of the Chupacabra strolling through a graveyard in Merrimack, New Hampshire, U.S.A. One of the eyewitnesses was a police officer who said the creature looked like something straight out of a horror movie.

THE THEORIES

MOST SCIENTISTS BELIEVE legendary Chupacabra sightings are the result of a case of mistaken identity. Because Chupacabras are said to be hairless, experts believe people are actually seeing coyotes plagued with mange. Sick coyotes are known to prey on domestic livestock, which is easier to catch than free-range prey—possibly explaining the "monster's" taste for goats and sheep.

But there are plenty of persistent people, like the eyewitnesses in New Hampshire, who believe the Chupacabra is a real monster.

Coyotes like this one are found all over North America. Could Chupacabra eyewitnesses have mistaken a sick or diseased coyote for the mysterious cryptid?

Loren Coleman, who runs the International Cryptozoology Museum in Portland, Maine, U.S.A., agrees that some of the sightings thought to be the Chupacabra are nothing more than sick coyotes—but he thinks there's more to the legend. He points to freakish details included in eyewitnesses' descriptions—like the red eyes, quills, and forked tongue—that make the creature sound more monstrous than just an under-the-weather coyote.

Others believe the Chupacabra is based more on fiction than on reality. In the summer of 1995, around the time of the first Chupacabra sightings, an alien movie was released in Puerto Rico. The aliens in the film were suspiciously similar to the original eyewitness accounts of the Chupacabra. Were people just freaked out by the movie monsters and letting their imaginations run wild? To add fuel to this freaky fire, around the same time, a newspaper in South America printed a far-fetched report suggesting that NASA had accidentally created the Chupacabra in a lab while they were conducting research on monkeys.

Is there any truth to these tales, or are they a bunch of monkey business? You'll have to decide for yourself—but it is enough to make anyone go bananas!

DID SCIENTISTS COOK UP THE CHUPACABRA IN A LAB WHILE DOING RESEARCH ON MONKEYS?

MOTHMAN

DON'T MESS WITH THIS MOTH!

THE BACKGROUND

POINT PLEASANT, WEST VIRGINIA, U.S.A., is a perfectly pleasing place—a small town at the junction of the Ohio and the Kanawha Rivers. But for 13 months starting in late 1966, life there wasn't pleasant at all when a terrifying tourist came to town. This is when witnesses first documented night-marish encounters with a petrifying flying semi-human beast. The debate about this winged wonder later inspired a movie, books, a museum, and a sculpture. So, who—or what—was this menacing man of nightmares? See if you think there's any fact behind this terrifying modern-day legend.

WEST VIRGINIA
UNITED STATES

OHIO   PENNSYLVANIA

Point Pleasant
WEST VIRGINIA
KY.   VIRGINIA

The **MOTHMAN** reportedly had **GLOWING RED EYES** and a terrifying 10-foot (3-m) wingspan.

THE DETAILS

REPORTS OF THIS CREATURE startled the town's residents and the local police. Because of his huge wingspan, the newspaper dubbed the nocturnal monster "Mothman." As reports of him surfaced, strange things started to happen in and around the town. Mysterious lights shot across the sky. Strange voices called out. Domestic animals dropped dead. Phones rang when they weren't plugged in. Witnesses' eyes burned. Then, in December of 1967, a local bridge collapsed, killing 46 people. Some people believed the arrival of Mothman foretold the disaster, especially since after the bridge tragedy the insect invader was never seen again.

THE CLUES
During the Mothman's time in Point Pleasant, more than 100 eyewitnesses reported seeing him. Many of the monster-spotters were respected members of the community. No matter how you look at this freaky flyer and the havoc it wreaked, the clues are sure to curdle your blood.

 DETAILED DESCRIPTIONS Most eyewitnesses had similar descriptions of the winged monstrosity. The Mothman stood about seven feet (2.1 m) tall on stocky legs and had heavy-duty wings like a large bird.

HIGH-SPEED CHASE In one of the first sightings of the Mothman, the creature reportedly flew after a car at speeds of up to 100 miles an hour (161 km/h)—faster than any known bird can fly—and made a high-pitched cry.

BIG BIRD Sandhill cranes are large North American birds that can stand more than three feet tall (1 m) and stretch their wings more than six feet (2 m) across. They're sometimes spotted near Point Pleasant.

After a local bridge collapsed, the Mothman was never seen again.

Sandhill cranes, which inhabit the area around Point Pleasant, are known to have huge wingspans. Could these beautiful birds flying at night have given rise to the Mothman sightings?

A STATUE OF MOTHMAN IN POINT PLEASANT, WEST VIRGINIA

AN EYEWITNESS SKETCH OF MOTHMAN

THE THEORIES

A WELL-KNOWN UFOLOGIST (someone who studies unidentified flying objects, or UFOs) named John Keel researched and wrote about the Mothman phenomenon extensively throughout his career. He conducted an intensive investigation, which included interviews with witnesses over two years. His conclusion? He believes the Mothman was real.

Some believers say the Mothman was the result of a curse uttered by a local Native American chief before he was killed by Revolutionary War soldiers in the area in 1777. These people point to Mothman's unbelievable speed as evidence of his otherworldly ability.

Still others believe in more natural explanations. Mothman skeptics claim the creature was simply a big bird—perhaps a local Sandhill crane—and that frightened eyewitnesses must have imagined the creature to be larger than life. Skeptics also dismiss the idea that the Mothman was responsible for the tragic bridge accident. Poor engineering, they say, likely caused the bridge to collapse: Opened in 1928, the aluminum bridge was prone to swaying and may have simply failed under a full load of cars and large trucks.

Today, you can visit a 12-foot (3.7-m)-tall stainless steel sculpture of the baffling big man in a park named after the legend in Point Pleasant. Whether fact or fiction, his infamous flybys brought a lot of attention to the small town.

MORE MYSTERIOUS MONSTERS

DID YOU KNOW that scientists discover thousands of new species every year? Between 2014 and 2017, more than 70,000 new creatures revealed themselves. There were cartwheeling spiders, a dwarf dragon, toothed frogs, and weird marine worms that resemble churros (a popular dessert made from fried dough). Some species are furry, some are friendly ... and some seem downright monstrous. Every so often, a new discovery seems to defy science, while capturing our wild imaginations. These include a hair blob that washed up on a beach in the Philippines and a chilling video from Alaska that seemed to capture a sea monster. These creepy creatures give us a lot of possibilities to ponder. Read on to find out more.

CHENA RIVER ICE
MONSTER

AN ALASKAN might-be monster was witnessed in 2016 when an employee of the Alaska Bureau of Land Management caught a frightening, frosty find on video: what appeared to be a creature (estimated to be 12 to 15 feet [3.6 to 4.5 m] long) slithering through the icy water of the Chena River in Alaska, U.S.A.! The video quickly went viral, and speculation spun out of control about what the object could be. Was it an ice monster, a giant zombie salmon, or is there a perfectly rational explanation? In 2016, the Alaska Department of Fish and Game announced that it was in fact just an ice-covered rope attached to a pier. It looks like this tale's at the end of its rope.

MEGALODON

THIS MYSTERIOUS MEGA-SHARK might seem like science fiction, but it really swam the world's oceans from about 16 million to 2 million years ago. These enormous sharks grew to be more than 50 feet (16 m) long, or about the length of a tractor-trailer. Megalodon likely had a more powerful bite than a *T. rex*. A grown man could have stood upright in its ginormous jaws. Scientists today think that changing ocean conditions brought about their extinction. And though some say these huge sharks could still lurk in the ocean depths, most scientists agree that idea is more scary science fiction than fact.

MOKELE-MBEMBE

SOME PEOPLE think Nessie (page 10) is actually a prehistoric marine reptile that eluded extinction after the time of the dinosaurs. Well, if Nessie could survive, what about other dinosaurs? Deep in the heart of Africa, in a remote area of the Congo, there is a legend about a lake creature called "Mokele-mbembe," which translates to "one who stops the flow of water" and "mysterious monster" in the local language. This legendary creature's description matches that of a sauropod, a giant plant-eating dinosaur with a long neck. Legend has it that Mokele-mbembe roars like a lion and has the power to kill an elephant with a single stab of its horn. Lots of people have claimed to see Mokele-mbembe, but so far proof of this magnificent monster is as elusive as the creature itself.

TULLY MONSTER

THIS MONSTROUS MYSTERY of science had a big pincer at the end of a long nose, eyes on stalks, and a tail like a shovel. Scientists aren't even sure which way was up for this ancient swimming torpedo, discovered when a fossil was found in a creek in Illinois, U.S.A., in 1955. What's even weirder is that paleontologists couldn't figure out how to classify it: They all think it swam in rivers more than 300 million years ago, but that's where the agreement ends. Some say it was a fish called a lamprey. Others strongly disagree. It's been called a worm, argued to be a mollusk, and compared to sea slugs and lobsters.

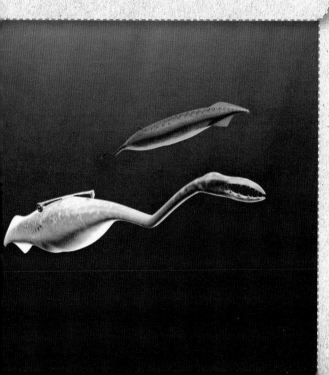

BIGFOOT

THEY DON'T MAKE SHOES BIG ENOUGH FOR *THESE* FAR-OUT FEET!

WARNING
BIGFOOT
IN THIS AREA

THE BACKGROUND

1 **THE CRANKY CRYPTID** known as Bigfoot first made big news in 1958 when a construction worker in Northern California found a massive 17.5-inch (44.5-cm) footprint from an unidentified creature. He made a cast of the print and word got around. Ever since, the public has been chomping at the bit to catch a glimpse of the massive hairy beast called Bigfoot, said to prowl remote and rocky regions of North America. Legends of other giant furry cryptids from around the world seem to make Bigfoot more credible. There's the Abominable Snowman in the Himalaya, the yeti in Tibet, and the yowie in Australia. It's as if they all come from the same monstrous family. So is there any truth to these stories? Are there huge, shy ape-like beings hiding in the hills of North America?

Most experts remain skeptical. But still, so many eyewitness accounts are hard to ignore ...

THE DETAILS

2 **MANY PEOPLE** claim to have laid eyes on Bigfoot. He's tall. He's scary. He's brown and furry and probably doesn't smell great. Also known as Sasquatch, he beats his chest with powerful arms, has a roaring growl, and emits blood-curdling screams. Myth and legends about this elusive and fearsome monster have persisted for centuries. Besides gigantic footprints, a few fuzzy images of the 10-foot (3-m)-tall, 400-pound (181-kg) creature exist. Believers say that this is evidence that proves Bigfoot is real. But are they the real deal?

THE THEORIES

3 **IN 1967,** an amateur filmmaker named Roger Patterson visited the area where the original footprint had been found in California, hoping to catch the creature on film. He claims he did: The video footage he captured that day shows a muscular and tall ape-like figure walking near a creek, but the authenticity of the film has been debated, scrutinized, and cross-examined for decades.

IS THAT YOU, BIGFOOT?

Many believe Bigfoot is a hoax. While plenty of people have claimed to see him, there are no good photos or clear film footage, and no bones or other physical evidence have ever been found that were scientifically proven to be from the big guy. Over the years, countless footprints have been revealed to be fakes. In 2008, someone claimed to have discovered the dead body of a Bigfoot, but it turned out to be a frozen rubber ape suit.

In 2015, genetic analyses of 18 sure-thing Sasquatch specimens revealed that the specimens belonged to raccoons, sheep, black bears, porcupines, horses, dogs, deer, and cows.

Yet some still believe in the existence of the hairy humanoid, including a few scientists. They think there might be thousands of these hairy heavyweights roaming around in the woods of North America, living off berries and fruit. We may never know for sure, but if you're up north out in the woods, keep your camera handy and be prepared to make a quick exit.

NEW EVIDENCE REVEALED!

In 2017, a team of scientists reinvestigated the 1967 Patterson video that has been the most significant evidence supporting the existence of Bigfoot. Patterson believed he saw Bigfoot. And it was a close encounter ... so close that he claimed to have seen the monster's rippling muscles as it walked away. The scientists attempted to re-create Bigfoot's peculiar walk as seen in the footage to investigate whether or not it was real or a person walking in disguise. A high-resolution digital microscope enabled the researchers to "de-fuzz" the grainy original video and get a better look at the creature's face. Their findings convinced some members of the team that the Bigfoot caught on film could be real. Others thought it was a hairy hoax. What do you make of this monstrous body of evidence?

VANISHING

ACTS

THROUGHOUT THE COURSE OF HISTORY, many cultures and civilizations have come and gone. But when a group of people thrives for thousands of years and then—poof!—disappears, leaving behind their homes, their art, and their inventions, it makes you wonder: What happened? Archaeologists and other scientists do everything they can to decode messages written centuries ago, piece together fragile bones hidden under layers of dirt, or literally get their feet wet diving to discover more clues.

THE NASCA LINES INCLUDE SOME 70 ANIMAL AND PLANT DESIGNS, INCLUDING THIS ANIMAL, WHICH EXPERTS BELIEVE IS A HUMMINGBIRD.

THE CITY OF ÇATALHÖYÜK

STONE-AGE RESIDENTS PIONEERED FARMING BUT **ROLLED OUT** BEFORE THE WHEEL WAS INVENTED.

THE BACKGROUND

DURING THE STONE AGE, humans survived for millions of years by using tools made of—you guessed it—stone. They were nomads, meaning they moved from place to place in search of food. They hunted woolly mammoths, speared fish, and gathered eggs and berries. But late in the Stone Age, some ancient people settled down to farm in the same place season after season. They domesticated sheep and goats; planted crops like wheat, peas, and barley; and lived in tight-knit communities. One of these civilizations, called Çatalhöyük (sounds like cha-TAHL-hoo-yook), thrived for about 2,000 years (from around 7500 to 5700 B.C.) before its people mysteriously disappeared. Why did these famous farmers drop off the radar screen of history? The questions have archaeologists digging for clues and scratching their heads.

EUROPE
TURKEY
ASIA
AFRICA

BULGARIA Black Sea GEORGIA

GREECE

TURKEY
Çatalhöyük

SYRIA
IRAQ

Mediterranean Sea

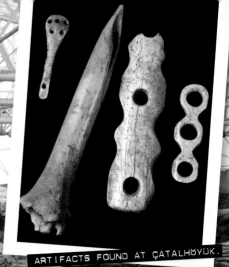

ARTIFACTS FOUND AT ÇATALHÖYÜK.

The people of Çatalhöyük had a grave ritual:
BURYING their dearly departed
loved ones under their homes!

the modern-day site of
Çatalhöyük in Turkey

THE DETAILS

ARCHAEOLOGIST JAMES MELLAART discovered the remnants of Çatalhöyük in 1952 on a marshy plateau in what is now central Turkey. The town was made up of a huge cluster of mud-brick houses over an area about as big as 50 football fields. It was one of the world's biggest cities for its time and home to as many as 10,000 prehistoric people.

But these were not your average city dwellers. They had some bizarre habits, even by ancient standards. They built their houses so close together that there was little room to move between them. People moved around on rooftops and descended by ladders into homes. Forget the front door; neighbors literally dropped in for a visit! Their civilization thrived for thousands of years and then ... the inhabitants disappeared. So what happened to the people of this ancient city?

THE CLUES

Experts have found clues about the fate of Çatalhöyük's residents using a combination of modern technology, including ground-penetrating radar, and old-fashioned techniques, like digging out 10,000-year-old pieces of pottery, carved figurines, and human bones. Here are a few things they've discovered that clue us in to what might have happened to this mysterious community.

- **MOUND OF EVIDENCE** The discovery of a mound of ruins to the west of Çatalhöyük shows that the civilization might have expanded into the "suburbs" late in its history.

- **SICK DAYS** DNA analysis of ancient bones and teeth from Çatalhöyük residents hints that contagious and deadly diseases like tuberculosis might have swept through the civilization.

- **COLD SNAP** Based on studies of ancient weather patterns, some scientists believe that during the time of Çatalhöyük, in the 6000s B.C., Earth had a major cooling-off period that caused a severe drought in the area.

THE THEORIES

BRITISH ARCHAEOLOGIST IAN HODDER, who has studied the dusty site for decades, believes the end of Çatalhöyük may have been related to simple growing pains. The people started out farming goats and sheep, but excavated bones show that at some point they probably domesticated wild cattle, which need a lot of land for grazing. People may have expanded to new areas, like the site discovered west of the city, for more room.

WATERCOLOR PAINTING OF ÇATALHÖYÜK VILLAGE LIFE

ÇATALHÖYÜK GOLD FIGURE

Other experts say that Çatalhöyük was just one in a pattern of Stone Age cities that boomed and then collapsed. The likely culprit? Deadly germs. With so many people and animals living so close together—and no knowledge of how disease moves from person to person—fatal illnesses could have spread like wildfire.

Others point to changes in climate. In this case, it was likely a "cold drought" caused by glacial lakes draining into the ocean that left these folks out in the cold and low on water. Crops and livestock might have died, leaving the people to starve to death. Then there's the nearby volcano. Volcanic rock found at Çatalhöyük suggests that an ancient volcano called Mount Hasan blew during Çatalhöyük's time. If it did, it could have sent citizens seeking a different place to live—maybe one with less ash and hot lava.

Did one of these disaster scenarios put an end to Çatalhöyük? Perhaps it was something else that hasn't even been discovered yet. Experts may still dig up the truth about what happened to this super civilization.

STONE CARVING
FROM ÇATALHÖYÜK

NASCA GEOGLYPHS

DID MYSTERIOUS LINES SERVE AS **LANDING STRIPS FOR INCOMING** ALIEN **SPACECRAFT?**

Traces of **FOOTPRINTS** left by ancient artists can still be seen along some of the **NASCA GEOGLYPHS.**

THE BACKGROUND

IF YOU LOOK OUT THE WINDOW of your airplane while flying over the desert of southern Peru, you might think your eyes are deceiving you. But no, your eyes aren't deceiving you—those really are huge drawings scraped into the dry red desert below. Enormous animal images, like a life-size whale, a huge spider, a 1,000-foot (305-m) pelican, and a hummingbird with the wingspan of a jumbo jet, are called the Nasca lines. Also called geoglyphs, these drawings were etched into the desert more than 2,000 years ago. Thanks to an extremely dry climate (it rains only about an inch [25 mm] per year in the area), the supersize artwork has remained for centuries, even though the Nasca people vanished long ago.

These mysterious shapes have puzzled archaeologists, anthropologists, and anyone fascinated by weird ancient stuff since these forms were discovered in the late 1930s. That's when commercial planes first passed over the area and surprised passengers spotted the drawings. After the discovery, a mountain of questions emerged. What happened to the people who created these famous shapes? And what was the meaning and purpose of their ancient art?

The Nasca lines are one of archaeology's greatest mysteries because there are so many of them and they are so huge.

THE DETAILS

EXPERTS THINK that the Nasca people survived for about eight centuries, starting around 200 B.C. The art they left behind includes more than 800 straight lines and 300 geometric figures, including quadrangles, trapezoids, spirals, and long skinny lines—one is nine miles (14.5 km) long! The shapes cover an area measuring about 37 miles (59.6 km) long and one mile (1.6 km) wide. Creating them was no doubt an enormous undertaking. But what was the point of the grand-scale artwork left behind by this lost civilization?

THE CLUES

Though the mysterious glyphs' function is uncertain, one thing is for sure: The Nasca people made a lot of these long-lasting etchings. More than 1,000 of the pieces still exist today. Here are some clues that they hold:

- **STAR-STUDDED** In the 1940s, an American professor noticed that the sunset aligned with the Nasca line he was standing near, fueling a hunch that the lines had something to do with astronomy.

- **RAIN DANCE** Climate data suggests that around A.D. 500 a series of droughts devastated the previously fertile valley where the Nasca had flourished.

- **SYMBOLIC SIGNS** In ancient Peruvian culture, spiders are known to be a sign of rain, and hummingbirds symbolize fertility.

WHY DID THE NASCA PEOPLE LEAVE, AND WHERE DID THEY GO?

THE PRESENT-DAY FERTILE NASCA VALLEY REGION IN PERU

THE THEORIES

FOR ALMOST 100 YEARS, people have tried to figure out the true purpose of the mysterious Nasca geoglyphs. One early theory was that they were an astrological calendar created in alignment with the stars. Later, some suggested that they served a purpose that was even more out of this world—guiding alien spacecraft to land on Earth. (Of course, there's no evidence to support that far-out theory.)

In the 1970s, researchers theorized that the lines had more to do with the desert they were carved into. In times of drought, the Nasca people would have been desperate for water. Instead of the lines pointing to celestial targets, one theory is that the lines and shapes led to an ancient source of water. A theory similar to that one is that the lines could have caught rainwater and funneled it to crops, like an artistic irrigation system.

National Geographic Explorer and archaeologist Johan Reinhard believes that serious drought conditions inspired the Nasca to create many of the geoglyphs as a plea to the gods for help. They may have thought that some symbols had the power to change the weather, and others the power to bring wilting crops back to life.

As for what happened to the Nasca people, many experts say the dry climate that inspired (and preserved) the artwork might also have brought an end to the civilization. If the rivers ran dry and wars raged over what water did remain, it might have spelled trouble for these mysterious grand-scale sketchers. We may never know what the ancient Nasca were up to when they created this long-lasting artwork, but one thing is for sure: People are still lining up hoping to solve this marvelous mystery.

GREAT ZIMBABWE

IN ITS OWN TIME, THIS PLACE MAY HAVE BEEN AFRICA'S GLITZIEST CITY.

THE BACKGROUND

SINCE THE DAWN OF HUMANKIND, the ability to trade goods and services has helped people survive and civilizations thrive. Today, we have great skyscraping cities like New York, London, and Tokyo that serve as hot spots for managing trade of an endless list of goods from bubble gum to basketballs, from rice to rubber tires. But back in the 13th century, the world's great trading cites weren't all shiny metal and sparkling glass. In the 1870s, a German explorer discovered the remains of what could have been an ancient stone super-city on a windswept plain in southern Africa. It's called Great Zimbabwe. Could it really have been one of the world's grandest cities of its time?

AFRICA
ZIMBABWE

ZAMBIA

ZIMBABWE

MOZAMBIQUE

Great Zimbabwe

BOTSWANA

SOUTH
AFRICA

The ruins of Great Zimbabwe hint at its history of having once been a thriving city.

Great Zimbabwe's **TALLEST WALL** consists of as many as one million bricks held TOGETHER by nothing but gravity.

ANCIENT WALL AT GREAT ZIMBABWE

THE DETAILS

EXPERTS THINK Great Zimbabwe could have been an important trading center during the Middle Ages. Merchants could have traveled there from as far away as Portugal, Egypt, and India. They would have brought beads and cloth to barter for valuables like gold, rhino horns, tortoise shells, and ivory. The remains of this great city span about 1,800 acres (728 ha). According to some experts, clues left behind hint that the site once held a magnificent city, complete with a palace and stone fortresses full of gems and gold. But just how great was Great Zimbabwe?

THE CLUES

Artifacts left behind give us plenty of prospects for figuring out just how great Great Zimbabwe really was. Take a read and see what you can glean from these glittering clues:

- **GOING FOR GOLD** The site of Great Zimbabwe is surrounded for miles by ancient gold mines.

- **RITZY RELICS** Immaculate sculptures, gold and copper coins, beads, and porcelain are among the treasures found in the ruins of Great Zimbabwe.

- **FANCY FEASTS** Nearly 150,000 pieces of cattle bones were found in the area around Great Zimbabwe.

Historians are still searching for answers about the origin and purpose of Great Zimbabwe. African legend says the place was a playground for giants.

THE THEORIES

ONE THEORY about Great Zimbabwe is that it was literally a golden city, situated directly between gold-producing regions nearby and coastal ports, like modern-day Mozambique. Some archaeologists think gold was the secret behind Great Zimbabwe's greatness. For 300 years, two-fifths of the world's gold was traded through this region. In addition to gold, archaeological excavations of Great Zimbabwe have revealed riches like copper coins, glass beads,

ANCIENT EAGLE
CARVING

porcelain from China and Persia, and Arabian coins. For some experts, that proves that the place was a great international trading hub and a center of wealth.

Some say that Great Zimbabwe not only glittered with gold but was huge. At its height, Great Zimbabwe might have been home to more than 10,000 people. Experts believe that the rulers of this lost city governed an empire that stretched across most of modern day Zimbabwe (which means "house of stone" in one local language) and parts of Mozambique. All those people went through a lot of food—and the bones from their meals survived to prove it. Bones from choice cuts of meat were found within the biggest stone fortresses, suggesting that the leaders and the richest citizens probably resided within the fortress walls.

As for why the civilization disappeared, no one knows for sure. Some experts think the gold that fueled the city ran out, and its people had to abandon their homes and set out to find new fortunes. As for whether it really was Africa's golden city—well, that's a secret worth its weight in gold.

LEAVE NO STONE UNTURNED TRYING TO FIGURE OUT WHAT HAPPENED TO THIS MOUNTAIN OF A MYSTERY.

THE BACKGROUND

A BEAUTIFUL TOWER, tall and slender, looms over a barren mountain desert. Called a minaret, it's decorated with turquoise tile and stretches 200 feet (61 m) up toward the sky, just like it has for more than eight centuries. It may have been a landmark in a legendary city called Firuzkuh (sounds like fee-ROOZ-coo). If the legends are true, the fabulous city was the summer capital of the massive Ghurid Empire, which stretched from present-day Iran to India. But it existed for less than a century. So what happened to this awesome oasis? How could it have vanished, leaving just the turquoise tower to mark the spot? Flip the page to see what you can piece together about this awesome ancient ruin.

ASIA
AFRICA
AFGHANISTAN
TAJIKISTAN
Turquoise Mountain
IRAN
AFGHANISTAN
PAKISTAN

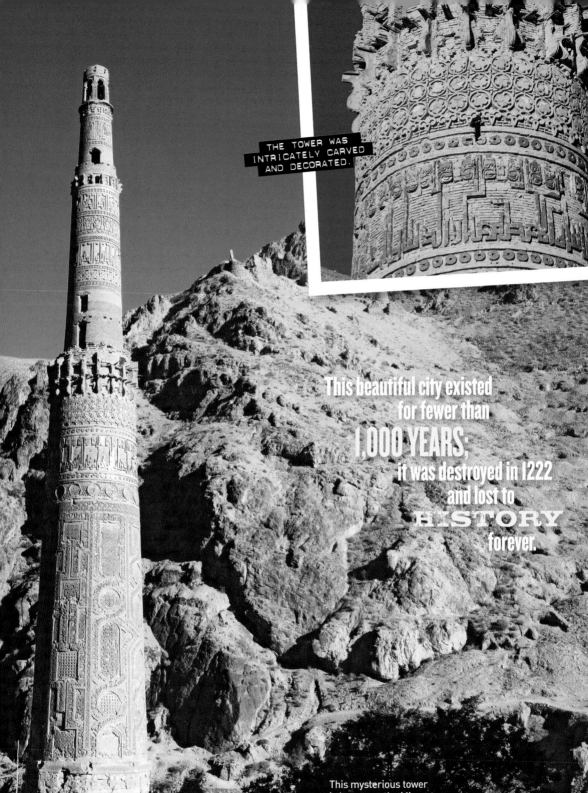

THE TOWER WAS INTRICATELY CARVED AND DECORATED.

This beautiful city existed for fewer than 1,000 YEARS; it was destroyed in 1222 and lost to HISTORY forever.

This mysterious tower is known as the Minaret of Jam and was built with baked bricks.

THE DETAILS

THE MINARET STANDS SOLO, surrounded by mountains that stretch nearly 8,000 feet (2,438 m) toward the sky, in one of the most remote and beautiful areas of Afghanistan. Made of baked rocks, tile, and stucco, the structure displays intricate geometric designs and Arabic calligraphy. It's one of the country's most ancient treasures and is thought to have been part of a long-lost mosque that was used as a platform to call people to prayer. It was built in the 1100s in the heyday of what archaeologists believe was a cosmopolitan city located at the rocky gorge where two rivers, the Jam and the Hari, meet. What secrets are these mountains keeping?

THE CLUES

What else is there to know about this intriguing big blue tower? Here's what experts have unearthed:

➜ **FLOODED FINDS** Next to the tower, archaeologists have found evidence of an ancient courtyard with river sediment covering its paving stones.

➜ **SMOKE SIGNALS** Inside the tower, steep steps rise more than 100 feet (30 m), leading to a circular chamber. Beams in the ceiling of the room appear blackened by smoke.

THE THEORIES

SOME SAY THE CITY was destroyed by a violent storm. Since two rivers flowed very close to the site, floods were a constant threat. Flash floods as a result of heavy rain could have washed away the mosque, or place of worship, that was once attached to the minaret.

Others say the legendary city, Firuzkuh, which may have been a famous capital city in the Middle Ages, was destroyed by Genghis Khan, the ruthless Mongolian ruler who lived from 1162 to 1227 and plotted to take over all of northeast Asia by defeating every tribe in the area.

Over the past 10 years, pillagers have looted and damaged what's left of the site. They dug up and sold all the artifacts they could find, leaving almost no evidence for experts to work with. This is one mystery whose secrets may stay lost forever.

STATUE OF GENGHIS KHAN

LOCATED IN AFGHANISTAN'S GHOR PROVINCE, THE TOWER SITS ON THE HARI RIVER.

DETAIL WORK
ON THE TOWER'S
FACADE

45

LOST CITY OF PAITITI

IS THIS LOST GOLDEN CITY AN UNDISCOVERED TROVE OF TREASURE ... OR FOOL'S GOLD?

THE BACKGROUND

1 **DEEP IN THE AMAZON JUNGLE,** there's a secret. Legend has it that there's a city made of gold buried somewhere beneath the rain forest's thick green canopy. Explorers have dubbed it the Lost City of Paititi. The Lost City has long been an attraction for explorers, archaeologists, and treasure seekers. The place is said to have been built with gold: The buildings were made of solid gold bricks, and the streets were even paved with the stuff. It's an enticing bit of lore that would have any would-be treasure seeker's heart racing. Nobody knows exactly where this golden city is—that is, if it ever existed at all. But experts have discovered a few nuggets of information that have lead to some sparkling theories.

THE DETAILS

2 **LEGEND HAS IT THAT THE INCAS** built the Lost City as a safe refuge after the Spanish took over much of the area in the 1500s. The actual location of the coveted city has been disputed: Some say it's in southeastern Peru; others say southwestern Brazil; still others say northern Bolivia. But all agree it's deep in the jungle, isolated, and hard to reach. Although many people have searched these areas, none have struck gold. But that doesn't mean the Lost City is a hoax: It could just be well concealed. The vast Amazon rain forest spans many South American countries and contains thousands of rivers and almost 400 billion trees—all things that could easily cover even a flashy city made of gold.

THE THEORIES

③ **IF YOU LISTEN** to the tales of the legend, it might seem that there are as many "lost cities" in South and Central America as there are jungles. Many explorers over the centuries have claimed to have discovered the ruins of this particular lost city. In 1600, a missionary reported that he had seen a large golden city in the region where Paititi is believed to have been built. In 2008, researchers found ruins of an ancient fortress in the area that local officials claimed was the Lost City.

French explorer Thierry Jamin has trekked into the Amazon through rugged terrain and up and down steep, remote mountains on 20 expeditions during the past 20 years in search of Paititi. In 2012, he zeroed in on a remote mountain area in Peru's protected Megantoni National Sanctuary. He and his team used satellite images to zoom in on a mountain with an oddly shaped top that they'd

WAS THIS LEGENDARY CITY FILLED WITH RICHES?

GOLD ARTIFACT DEPICTING THE OPULENCE OF AN ANCIENT CITY OF GOLD

heard about from locals. Close by, there was a lake and four reservoirs carved out of the jungle that had a peculiar human-made look to them.

NEW EVIDENCE REVEALED!

THIS AREA IS SO HARD TO REACH that efforts to get there have stalled investigations over the years. But Jamin and a team of researchers plan to target the square-topped mountain soon. They are determined to see if the site might hide the remains of the Lost City of Paititi. The place won't be easy to reach. It's so remote and deep in the Amazon that they'll have to fly in by helicopter and then drive 4x4 vehicles (packed with equipment, drones, and sophisticated sensing equipment) to the site. A team of archaeologists will spend weeks scouring the area. But people have been searching for this priceless place for 400 years—will this search for gold pan out?

3

UNEXPLAINED
OCCURRENCES

HAVE YOU EVER COME ACROSS SOMETHING so freaky that it boggled your brain? From a bizarre light blinking at Earth from 1,500 light-years away that some think is the work of aliens to mysterious mummies with obscure origins, this chapter is full of unexplainable occurrences that really happened—or are happening right now. Scientists and thrill seekers alike work day and night to try to figure out answers to these puzzlingly freaky phenomena. Read on for some bone-chilling, bloodcurdling cases that will make you question everything you thought you knew.

ANSWERS TO THIS ARCTIC MYSTERY HAVE BEEN ON ICE FOR MORE THAN 150 YEARS.

Sir John Franklin led a doomed expedition in 1845 that became one of the biggest mysteries of its century.

THE BACKGROUND

SINCE THE FIRST SHIPS SET SAIL on Earth's vast oceans, stormy voyages, shipwrecks, and sailors lost at sea have set the stage for great legends of the deep. But the tale of the Franklin expedition might be the most chilling nautical narrative of them all. It took place in the Arctic and involved not one missing ship, but two. And most frightening of all, the expedition was captained by a man rumored to have once eaten human flesh to survive a voyage gone wrong. Turn the page to discover all the details about the frozen fate of the Franklin expedition.

Captain **FRANKLIN** earned the nickname **"THE MAN WHO ATE HIS BOOTS"** after he and his crew ran out of food on an earlier Arctic expedition.

THE DETAILS

THIS ICY MYSTERY got underway in 1848 after two ships, H.M.S. *Erebus* and H.M.S. *Terror,* set out on what would become a doomed Arctic expedition. Their mission? To search for a sea route that connected the Atlantic Ocean and the Pacific Ocean through Arctic waters. The expedition started smoothly. But after the ships entered what's called Lancaster Sound (the eastern entrance of the route now known as the Northwest Passage), they sailed north and encountered impenetrable ice. Historians know that at some point the ships turned back, but neither of them was ever heard from again. The original search for the missing crews went on for 11 years, but during that time few clues were ever found. What happened when this wintry journey went south? The search for answers has sailed on for more than a century.

THE CLUES

Numerous expeditions searched for the lost Franklin expedition. But it wasn't until 2014 that Canadian researchers found the H.M.S. *Erebus.* Two years later, the H.M.S. *Terror* was found in the same area. But where were the crews? Here are some clues that have been chilling on ice:

- **NOTED** A note dated April 25, 1848, was concealed in a pile of rocks found in the Canadian Arctic on King William Island. The note said that *Erebus* and *Terror* had been stuck on sea ice and abandoned three days before.

- **ICE-CHEWED** In 2014, a helicopter pilot spotted a large iron object leaning against a rock in the same area where Inuit stories told of a sunken wooden ship. The iron piece turned out to be a winch (a machine for lifting heavy objects) from the *Erebus,* along with the ship's stern, which appeared to have been damaged by ice. The ship was almost perfectly preserved and discovered in shallow water nearby.

- **TRACES IN THE TUNDRA** Items such as a toothbrush and the tattered scrap of a uniform have been found along the barren ice fields.

AN ARTIST'S RENDERING SHOWING A SEARCH PARTY LOOKING FOR THE FRANKLIN EXPEDITION

THE THEORIES

MOST HISTORIANS agree that the two ships probably became trapped in heavy sea ice as they tried to sail back south. The crew—more than a hundred men— likely abandoned their ships in the waters off King William Island and tried to get out of the Arctic on foot after attempts to free the vessels failed. They are rumored to have set off south toward a trading post 600 miles (965 km) away, but it's likely they died from exposure to the freezing temperatures and starvation. The toothbrush and piece of uniform were likely lost along their tragic trek.

Most historians believe that Captain Franklin died before the crew abandoned the ships. According to Inuit oral histories, his body was found (along with a note) in his bedroom aboard the ship, his face sporting an eerie grin. As for what happened to his body, and the bodies of the crew, no one knows for sure.

Members of an 1880 search party take a rest at lunchtime while searching the Arctic for members of the ill-fated crew of the Franklin expedition.

THE LITTLE GREEN MEN ON MARS MIGHT HAVE NEW NEIGHBORS.

THE BACKGROUND

LOOK UP AT THE SKY on a clear night and you might see thousands of stars that make you wonder about hard-to-fathom distances and the possibility of mysterious aliens. One star, which isn't visible without a heavy-duty telescope, has astronomers mystified. It's called Tabby's Star, and it hangs way above the Milky Way, between the constellations Cygnus the swan and Lyra the harp. Observations have revealed some weird light shows coming from the star, and nobody can figure out exactly what's going on. Is this the work of some natural but so-far-unexplained occurrence in space, or is it possible that the cause is more—well—*alien* in nature? Flip the page for more star-studded details.

Cygnus, the swan nebula, where Tabby's Star is located

Tabby's Star may have "EATEN" a nearby PLANET—incinerating it and causing a SPECTACULAR light show.

THE DETAILS

THE QUESTIONS STARTED IN 2009 when NASA's Kepler mission embarked on a project to study planets outside of our solar system. Scientists focused a high-powered telescope on one field in the sky to continuously monitor the brightness of some 150,000 stars. It took in data every 30 minutes for four years. A team of 300,000 citizen planet hunters helped study the data by looking out for patterns that the computers might have overlooked. One of those folks spotted an unusual pattern of light coming from the star identified as KIC 8462852, which is about 20,000 times bigger than Earth. The discovery left a lot of scientists scratching their heads. Nobody knows for sure what's going on out there, but see what you think after investigating what we *do* know.

THE CLUES

The striking star in this intriguing case has provided lots of data but even more questions. A few white-hot tips give us a glimpse into this far-out mystery:

FREAKY FLUCTUATIONS A star usually brightens with age, but Tabby's Star has been fluctuating for long and short intervals since 1890. In 2011 and 2013, the star's light dimmed in especially dramatic patterns.

PILES OF PLANETS Whatever is causing the dimming, it's big. It would take at least 50 Jupiter-size objects lining up all of a sudden in front of Tabby's Star to mimic the decreases in light witnessed from Earth.

ONE OF A KIND Tabby's Star is the only star ever known to shine in these kinds of mysterious dimming patterns.

SPACE LABORATORY

ILLUSTRATION OF AN ASTEROID IMPACT

THE THEORIES

MOST ASTRONOMERS think there's a natural explanation for Tabby's Star's odd light patterns. Perhaps we're watching a black hole gobble the star. Or maybe its light is being blocked by some unknown object—like a huge planet or a band of intergalactic dust. But one expert says these theories are full of hot gas.

Astronomer Tabetha Boyajian, who led the project that first discovered the star—and is the person for whom the star is named—wonders if the cause of the strange light patterns isn't so natural after all. She wonders if there could be an alien civilization living on the star that's much more advanced than ours here on Earth. She imagines that they've exhausted the energy supply of their home planet and are trying to capture more energy from their host by launching massive solar panel-like structures into orbit.

She thinks these structures—if they exist—could be blocking the star's light as they orbit the star, causing the bizarre dimming pattern.

Boyajian has one more theory involving aliens: What if those lucky enough to watch this star just witnessed an interplanetary space battle that destroyed a planet? She thinks the swirling fragments of the smashed planet could be what's blocking the light.

As fun as the alien stories sound, more and more experts are leaning toward the idea that the mysterious dimming of Tabby's Star is caused by something much more ordinary: dust. A new study published in late 2017 reported that circumstellar dust—that's dust that orbits a star—is causing the extraordinary light show that's caught the attention of astronomers over the years. But we can't know for sure. The dust on this mega-mystery may never settle completely.

Massive amounts of swirling space dust and gas, as shown in this image from the European Space Agency's Herschel Space Observatory telescope, pinpoint areas of star formation.

WOW! SIGNAL

DiD ALIENS SEND US THIS MYSTERIOUS MIXED MESSAGE?

THE BACKGROUND

FROM SMOKE SIGNALS to status updates, people have been finding new and different ways to send messages since the beginning of time. But what if it turned out that humans aren't the only ones trying to get in touch? In the 1970s, SETI (Search for Extraterrestrial Intelligence) researchers detected a strange signal that many thought might be a message from the inhabitants of another galaxy. News of the signal created a cosmological mystery: What did it mean, and who did it come from? It had never happened before, and it has not happened since. To this day, the mystery is one of the most perplexing puzzles to ever stump science.

A large antenna dish in New Mexico, U.S.A., monitors the Milky Way galaxy, the enormous group of stars, gas, and dust that includes Earth.

The **WOW!** signal lasted about 72 seconds and has never been **DETECTED AGAIN.**

THE DETAILS

IN 1977, a telescope nicknamed "Big Ear" was searching the sky for incoming radio signals (specifically, communications from potential extraterrestrial civilizations) when it detected something truly odd. Volunteer observatory researcher Jerry Ehman was reviewing data from the telescope's scan that mid-August day. That's when he noticed something strange. Amid endless columns and rows of numbers that represent the intensity of a radio signal, he discovered a sudden burst of activity—an obvious outlier amid the standard radio signals the telescope usually picked up. He grabbed a pen, circled the numbers, and wrote "Wow!" The signal was forever called the Wow! signal.

THE CLUES
The Wow! signal was the loudest, longest signal that the telescope ever picked up during its career. But details about where the signal came from and what it means have kept astronomers and alien lovers guessing and pressing for answers for decades. Here's what we do know about the Wow! signal:

WOW! SIGNAL PRINTOUT

SOUNDING OFF The radio signal lasted 72 seconds, considered to be a long signal by experts. It was 30 times louder than most noise in space.

STAR-STUDDED The signal came from a location northwest of a globular cluster of stars called M55, in the constellation Sagittarius.

FULL OF GAS The signal had the same frequency as hydrogen, which is found in the gassy plume that follows a comet. Planets and other "natural" sources of these signals tend to send a much broader range of frequencies.

THE THEORIES

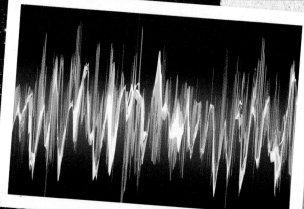

SOUND WAVES

DURING THE 1960S, Ehman and a group of Cornell physicists charted out their best guesses about how a faraway extraterrestrial civilization (if one did exist) might try to get in touch with its neighbors. They found that radio signals were the ideal choice because they are efficient and can travel long distances through space. So, the Wow! signal was exactly like what researchers predicted an alien message would be, if they ever detected one.

Over the years, researchers have worked to blast out other explanations—like the signal was caused by satellites, aircraft, or ground-based transmitters on Earth. When they traced the message back to its origins, experts found that it came from a location where there were apparently no stars or even a planet. If it was from aliens, they would have to have extremely sophisticated technology that we might not even be able to imagine.

In 2016, an American astronomer published a report suggesting that the signal may have been noise from the passing of two comets detected by the telescope Big Ear. As a comet nears the sun, its surface begins to melt, which results in a plume of gas (possibly made of hydrogen) trailing behind it.

But some scientists are skeptical. They say if a comet caused the signal, we'd have heard something similar to it before or again. We may never know who or what sent that message, but we're waiting for the follow-up call.

This cluster of stars (left), called M55, is where scientists think the Wow! signal originated. It contains some 100,000 stars and is more than 17,600 light years from Earth!

WORLD HISTORY PUTS THESE WELL-PRESERVED PEEPS IN THE WRONG TIME AT THE WRONG PLACE.

THE BACKGROUND

THE COLOR OF OUR EYES, our hair, and our skin tell a story about who we are and where our ancestors came from. But what if the story doesn't add up? Early in the 20th century, archaeologists made an astonishing find at the edge of the hot Taklamakan Desert in northwestern China. Buried in the Tarim River Basin near a dry riverbed were about 200 naturally mummified bodies with blonde or red hair, blue eyes, and Western features. And they sported artifacts and tools that would not be seen in use in China for many years. So, if these ancient folks weren't of Chinese descent, who were they? Flip the page to see what you can figure out from details dug up from the grave.

ASIA
CHINA

RUSSIA
MONGOLIA
Tarim Basin
CHINA
INDIA

VILLAGE OF TUYUGOU

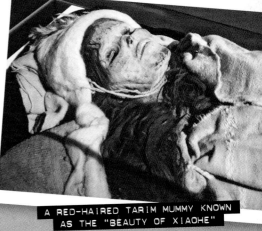

A RED-HAIRED TARIM MUMMY KNOWN AS THE "BEAUTY OF XIAOHE"

One of the Tarim **MUMMIES**
wears the oldest known pair of
PANTS
in the world.

TAKLAMAKAN DESERT

THE DETAILS

ANCIENT TEXTS tell stories of fair-haired people who had survived living in the desert of western China for more than a millennium, about 4,000 years ago. Since there was no hard evidence that any Caucasian people settled outside of the Western world that far back in world history, scholars dismissed them as myths. But could those old stories be true? And if so, where in the world did these people come from?

THE CLUES

Many artifacts were left by the Tarim Basin people. Scientists have been able to extract DNA from their well-preserved bodies to track down some answers surrounding these mysterious people and their origins. Here are a few clues to figure out this body of scientific work:

FASHION FINDS Many of the mummies were well-dressed in fine woolen textiles, with threads woven in diagonal patterns and plaids, and, in some cases, decorated with goose feathers.

TOOL TALK Fragments of bronze tools have been found with the Tarim mummies.

HORSE PLAY A mummy that researchers called the Cherchen Man was buried near a saddle and a horse skull. Other artifacts found in the burial site include part of a bridle and a horse hoof.

CHINESE SCRIPT

THE THEORIES

THE TARIM MUMMIES have provided scientists with a forensic investigation of epic proportions. Ancient artifacts and 4,000-year-old DNA molecules have helped rehydrate this dried-out case. One Harvard anthropologist who is an expert in ancient textiles believes the group may have started in Europe and migrated east, based on their clothing. Their fur-lined skirts, wool capes, and felt hats connect the dots to what people wore in Europe at the time. Other details that support this theory are hidden in the construction of the Tarim mummies' belts, boots, and fabric patterns, which can be traced to similar samples of that period from Germany, Austria, and Scandinavia.

Other research has focused on the fragments of bronze tools found with some of the mummies. In its time, bronze (copper combined with other metals and then heated and shaped into tools and ornaments) was one of the greatest inventions of human history. It's thought to have been first used in Mesopotamia about 6,000 years ago. Since bronze tools weren't known to appear in China until about 1,000 years later, some experts are convinced that the people of the Tarim Basin brought bronze tools when they traveled from Mesopotamia.

Some think the equine artifacts, like the saddle and horse skull, might link the Tarim Basin people to Western Siberia. People of this area are known to have been the first to domesticate horses, as early as 5,500 years ago. Were the mummies part of a nomadic tribe of horseback riders that spread to China from the plains of eastern Europe, long before other cultures were using horses?

In 2007, a National Geographic team analyzed DNA samples from the mummies to pinpoint the genetic origins of these people. The results were literally all over the map. The mummies had a wide variety of genetic backgrounds from Eurasia to Siberia. Their results suggest that the Tarim Basin could have been a kind of urban center where people from many different cultures and nationalities crossed paths and came to trade goods and services. And then, like many great mysteries, that hopping crossroad disappeared into the dust, leaving us to sleuth out the details of its history and the people who lived there, one clue at a time.

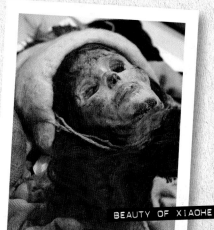

BEAUTY OF XIAOHE

MUMMY OF YINGPAN MAN

BLACK HOLES

THESE STAR-EATERS GOBBLE GASES, COMETS, AND EVEN LIGHT.

THE BACKGROUND

AT THE CENTER OF OUR GALAXY lurks something dark, mysterious—and with a seemingly insatiable appetite. It waits to pull in anything that crosses its horizon, from planets to space dust to spaceships. Even light, the fastest thing in the universe, can't escape. It's a black hole, which forms when a giant star runs out of energy. When that happens, the star implodes, and extreme heat and intense gravity cause its center to collapse under its own weight. The implosion is called a supernova, and it squashes the star into a very powerful speck. Imagine a magician waving his wand and a mountain-size hunk of iron becomes a highly magnetic grain of sand. That's a black hole (which you now know is not really a hole but a very tightly packed spot in space). But scientists know little about this freaky phenomenon: Some aren't even convinced black holes are real. Blast off onto the next page to read on and see what you make of it.

SAGITTARIUS A*,
the black hole at the center of the
MILKY WAY,
weighs more than FOUR
MILLION SUNS and can
tear a star apart.

an artist's concept of a
supermassive black hole

THE DETAILS

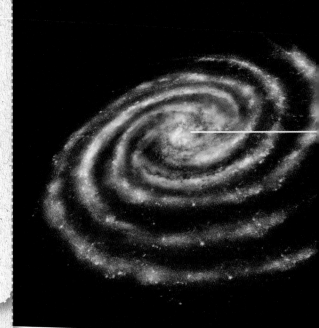

an artist's concept
depicting Sagittarius A*

A BLACK HOLE'S GRAVITY, or attractive force, is so strong that it pulls in anything within its reach, from dust to light, and even whole stars. Even though they're pretty much invisible against the black void of space, astronomers observe these strange space spots by measuring the effects black holes have on objects that get too close. They can watch as objects swirl toward the invisible black hole—until they disappear forever—like water down a drain. The first black hole was discovered in 1971, and, since then, scientists estimate our galaxy might hold about 100 million more. Here are some clues that have helped scientists determine whether black holes are fact or science fiction.

THE CLUES

The topic of black holes continues to fascinate experts and nonscientists alike. Here are a few clues astronomers have landed on to try to figure out how black holes work and if they really exist:

CENTER OF EVERYTHING In the 1960s, astronomers noticed that nearly every galaxy they observed seemed to be made up of dust, gas, and stars swirling around a single compact object.

RIGHTEOUS RIPPLES In 2016, a high-powered telescope in the United States magnified ripples in space-time that scientists think were created when two massive black holes smashed into each other more than a billion years ago.

INTERSTELLAR SELFIES After five nights of observations in April 2017, astronomers believed they had captured the first ever image of a black hole, creating a media frenzy.

ALBERT EINSTEIN

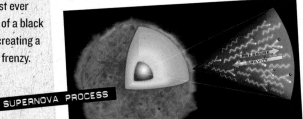

SUPERNOVA PROCESS

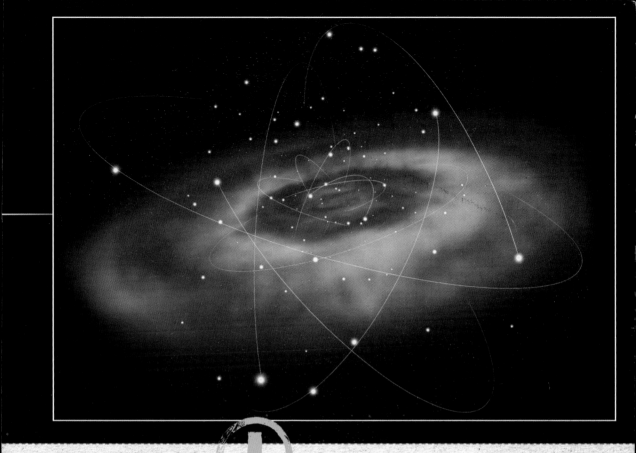

THE THEORIES

BY THE 1960S, scientists had developed new ways of seeing into space. That helped them confirm theories about the existence of black holes and how they form. X-ray and radio wave telescopes collected light in wavelengths that made it possible to see through interstellar dust and illuminate the bones of a galaxy (like the stars)—the same way a doctor might use an x-ray to see inside your body. What they saw was that each galaxy has a knot of space matter like stars and gas at its center, lumped around a heavy, dense object that experts could only explain as a black hole.

In 2016, the National Science Foundation announced that it had used extremely sensitive instruments to detect tiny vibrations from passing gravitational waves. This was a big deal and was the first time "gravitational waves" had ever been measured or heard on Earth. Those vibrations were clear evidence of a disturbance that had occurred three billion light years away when two ancient black holes collided and merged into one. These waves—the result of that ancient collision, which released what some experts say was the energy equivalent of a billion trillion suns—have given scientists more evidence that black holes exist.

In 2017, scientists tried to take the first ever photo of a black hole using the Event Horizon Telescope, a network of telescopes at radio astronomy centers on four continents so powerful it could spot a golf ball on the moon. The experts think they may have gotten the shot, but they have to sift through lots of data before they can be sure. One thing's for sure—there's a lot about these mysterious gravitational gargantuans left to be learned.

KING RICHARD III

WAS THIS ROYAL RUCKUS FOR REAL?

THE BACKGROUND

1 **THE HISTORY OF EUROPEAN** royalty is plagued with stories of greed, deception, and murder. But would a member of the royal family really go so far as to kill his young nephews to gain the throne? That's what some say happened with King Richard III. His nephew Edward V was next in line to be king. After Edward was his younger brother, Richard, Duke of York. But then both kings-to-be disappeared and Richard III assumed the throne. Was it a tragic coincidence, or was foul play to blame?

Here's what historians know for sure: Like a movie villain, Richard III is said to have been devilishly handsome with icy blue eyes. He did become king instead of his nephews, but he didn't reign for long. After Richard was killed in the bloody Battle of Bosworth in August 1485 at the age of 32, his body disappeared.

EDWARD V AND HIS BROTHER RICHARD OF SHREWSBURY

THE DETAILS

2 **THE SAGA STARTED** when the princes' father, King Edward IV, died. Richard III escorted the princes to the Tower of London, where Edward was to be crowned as king. But that's where the trail runs cold. The boys were never seen or heard from again, and Richard took the throne. The boys' deaths have remained one of Britain's most famous historical mysteries.

THE THEORIES

3 **MANY HISTORIANS SAY** King Richard III's bad reputation is pure fiction and that the tall tale was fueled by the medieval media. The hottest ticket in town at the time was famous playwright William Shakespeare's Richard III about—you guessed it—a king who murders his nephews to steal the throne and later dies in battle. Did the play inspire the legend of King Richard, or did his dastardly deeds inspire

the play? The jury's still out on that one.

Other experts believe Richard did kill his nephews, even without hard evidence, because he had so much power to gain from their deaths. Some think the evil king had them buried somewhere in the Tower of London, which was the last place they were seen alive.

In 1674, the bodies of two children were discovered in the tower. But to add another layer of mystery to this cold-blooded case, the Church of England has refused to carry out DNA testing that would indicate if the old bones belong to the missing royals.

Still others wonder if the young kings-to-be were killed at all, or if they could have been kidnapped. People have searched the tower up and down for more clues, but to this day, no one knows whether Richard was a loving uncle or a royal menace.

NEW EVIDENCE REVEALED!

IN 2012, archaeologists digging under a parking lot in Leicester, England, discovered skeletal remains. Genetic research (including DNA testing of living relatives of Richard III) revealed that the bones were his. The skeleton also revealed clues about the king's final moments, including his last meal, which experts think might have included peacock. The spot where the body was found was once the location of a monastery, a home where religious men lived. The skeleton had many gruesome battle wounds, including a blow to the head—which experts say is probably what killed Richard in battle 500 years earlier. After its discovery, the body was reburied with England's royalty. One thing the 2012 discovery didn't reveal: any evidence about what happened to the imperial nephews or whether or not their uncle was responsible for their deaths. That murderous mystery remains royally unsolved—for now.

4

STRANGE
SITES

FROM A GIANT HORSE etched into a hill to a waterfall that appears to be gushing blood, planet Earth is chock-full of stuff that defies explanation. These real-life places, things, and natural wonders are the strangest of them all—and what could be more fun than trying to unravel their mysteries? But these freaky phenomena hold on tight to their secrets. Turn the page to explore mysteries that are strange, sensational, and sometimes a little spooky.

For thousands of years, people have wondered how Egypt's Great Pyramids were built and why.

UFFINGTON WHITE HORSE

THIS SUPERSIZE STALLION IS SO HUGE IT CAN ONLY BE SEEN FROM ABOVE.

THE BACKGROUND

FOR CENTURIES, archaeologists, historians, and armchair detectives everywhere have puzzled over the giant horse outline cut into the chalky hills of what is today Oxfordshire, England. The figure stretches more than 330 feet (100 m) from nose to tail—about as long as 10 school buses in a row. This humongous horse has generated herds of questions: Who created this colossal carving, how did they do it, and why was it made in the first place? Trot on over to the next page to see what you make of this mega-mustang mystery.

UNITED KINGDOM EUROPE

AFRICA

ATLANTIC OCEAN

UNITED KINGDOM

North Sea

IRELAND

Uffington White Horse

FRANCE

People have been maintaining the Uffington White Horse— a giant, chalky artifact—for 3,000 years.

England has 56 **HILL FIGURES,**
including this divine
EQUINE,
plus giants and huge crosses.

THE DETAILS

THE UFFINGTON WHITE HORSE is the oldest hill figure (or geoglyph, like the Nasca lines on page 34) in Britain. To make it, ancient artists dug into the earth to expose the light-colored bedrock below. Centuries of regular grooming have kept the horse in tip-top shape. Every summer for the better part of 3,000 years, locals get together to "scour," or re-chalk, the figure.

THE CLUES

How in the world did this high horse come to be on this British hillside? Archaeologist and historians have been pondering this question for hundreds of years. Here are some clues they've been working with:

→ **PRETTY PENNY** Iron Age Celtic coins found in the region depict horses in the style of the Uffington horse image.

→ **FIRST DATE** A modern dating technique called optically stimulated luminescence pinpointed the last time bits of the horse's soil were exposed to light.

→ **BALD SPOT** The hillside near the Uffington White Horse bears a scar where no grass will grow.

Some say the Uffington White Horse is a dragon. Either way, these lines make up the animal's snout.

THE THEORIES

SCIENTISTS AND HISTORIANS have brought out ideas over the centuries about who created the horse and what it means. British archaeologist Gary Marshall says that in the 1800s, people believed the horse was some kind of enormous emblem made by the Anglo-Saxons, who lived in the area around 500 B.C. Then technology that emerged in the 1900s dated the horse back farther—to the Iron Age (between 1200 and 1000 B.C.). Iron Age coins cast with a similar horse image back up this theory.

But more recently, scientists have used cutting-edge scientific tools to test the ground at the site. They found that the Uffington White Horse is about 3,000 years old! Historians and archaeologists know that at that time a prehistoric Bronze Age tribe lived in the area. Their burial grounds can still be seen there today. Perhaps this group of people created the great horse to stake their claim to the area or to worship a god.

Still others claim the horse isn't a horse at all. Instead, they say it's a dragon. As evidence, they point to a low mound in the valley below the figure called "Dragon Hill" that has a strange bare area where no grass grows. Local legend says that long ago, a dragon was slain on the spot and its spilled blood has prevented things from growing there to this day.

Whether it's a flying fire-breather or just a giant horse, one mystery remains— how could anyone have created such a masterpiece without being able to see it from above? The answer may be lost to history.

VOLUNTEERS HELP MAINTAIN THE WHITE HORSE.

STRANGE
SECRETS
BUBBLE UP AT THIS
DEVILISH
HOT SPOT!

a painting depicting Cicero's villa
on the Bay of Baiae

THE BACKGROUND

IN A BARREN SPOT where a rocky, volcanic field meets the splashing surf of the Gulf of Naples, ancient Greek ruins hide a steamy secret. In the 1950s, a British amateur archaeologist named Robert Paget uncovered something strange while sifting through the dirt at an old vineyard near what is today Naples, Italy, a city on the Mediterranean Sea. It was an underground chamber—and when Paget and a few brave associates ventured inside, they discovered a series of narrow tunnels that looked like they hadn't been entered in a thousand years. Weirder still was the steamy 120°F (49°C) temperature. What exactly was this humid, hidden hotbed? Was this place a natural wonder, or a human-made gateway to a dark, hot underworld?

ATLANTIC OCEAN

EUROPE

ITALY

AFRICA

FRANCE

SWITZ.

I T A L Y

BOSN. & HERZ.

ALB.

Naples

Tyrrhenian Sea

Mediterranean Sea

Ionian Sea

TUNISIA

TEMPLE OF VENUS RUINS
AT BAIAE TUNNEL COMPLEX

A stream of **WATER**
that's hot to the touch runs under these
MYSTERIOUS
human-made tunnels.

THE DETAILS

IT TOOK YEARS of work for Paget and his team to clear the old passageways, which had been meticulously carved and then mysteriously filled with rubble. But once the tunnels were opened, this otherworldly warren revealed secret chambers, twisted tunnels, and gloomy dead ends. The tunnels led to a stream of natural boiling water, which explained the sizzling conditions—but heated up the mysterious nature of this superheated spot. Some secrets have been uncovered; others are still buried. So what on earth were these top secret tunnels use for?

THE CLUES

Historians, architects, and many other experts have traipsed through these tunnels trying to chisel out details about this dark mystery that dates back to the time of ancient Rome. Here are a few clues that they've found along the way:

➤ **IT'S A GAS** The tunnels have scorching temperatures, thick gaseous vapors, and a superheated stream, which make for one spooky site.

➤ **HEALING PLACE** Hidden staircases deep within the tunnel lead from ruins of water tanks to an area aboveground that may have been an ancient spa complex.

➤ **LIGHTS OUT** Niches carved into the tunnel every yard or so may have held ceremonial oil lamps.

The Baiae tunnels might have looked something like this.

ABOVEGROUND, THE AREA IS CLOUDED WITH SULFUR AND OTHER GASES.

AN ARTIST'S DEPICTION OF THE BATHS OF TRITOLI, NEAR BAIAE

THE THEORIES

TODAY, VOLCANIC RUBBLE AND RUINS of ancient temples dominate this spot. This site might look dormant, but its mysteries still run hot. One of the first theories to emerge was that the tunnels were dug by ancient Romans or Greeks who used the peculiar place to trick unwitting visitors. Using the choking gases and searing temperatures to their advantage, they might have swindled people by convincing them that the place was an entrance to a mythical underworld. Gullible, frightened guests might have paid to tour the tunnels—or perhaps to be shown the way out.

Another theory says the Baiae tunnels weren't built to scare, but to soothe: They could have delivered hot water to a spa above. The area was known for its popular spas for bathing and healing that existed thousands of years ago. Soaking in the mineral-rich water and breathing the gas vapors wafting up from underground was said to improve health and reduce pain.

Other people say the design of the place reflects rituals or ceremonial grounds. Niches carved into the tunnel likely held lamps, but some experts say there are far more niches than one would need just to light the place up. They think the lamps were used in some kind of ancient underground ceremonies. No matter what theory makes the most sense to you, this heated mystery may never cool off.

GIANT SPHERES OF COSTA RICA

THIS **MYSTERIOUS** CASE HAS GONE **STONE** COLD.

This carved rock, one of Costa Rica's mysterious stone spheres, was found in the village of Palmar Sur.

THE BACKGROUND

IN THE OPENING SCENE of the popular treasure-hunting thriller *Raiders of the Lost Ark,* a rocking, rolling, bouncing stone ball nearly crushes the movie's main character, Indiana Jones. The ball in the movie was a convincing work of fiction, but Costa Rica's mysterious stone spheres are real. Thousands of these very old and heavy stone balls can be found all over Costa Rica, from the country's jungles to its beaches. Many scientists have tried to figure out the riddle of these rocks, but so far these stones aren't talking. So ... who made these spectacular spheres, when, and why?

NORTH AMERICA

ATLANTIC OCEAN

COSTA RICA

PACIFIC OCEAN

SOUTH AMERICA

NICARAGUA

Caribbean Sea

COSTA RICA

PACIFIC OCEAN

PANAMA

Diquis Delta

A ROW OF THE STONE SPHERES

These **STONE SPHERES** range from the size of a **GOLF BALL** to one that is eight feet (2.4 m) wide and weighs **16 tons** (14.5 t).

THE DETAILS

THE SPHERES were first discovered in the 1930s when farmers began clearing land to make room for planting bananas. Instead of fertile fields, they uncovered about 300 rocky globes. The spheres are made from hard igneous river rocks, and many are clustered in the country's biologically rich Diquis Delta region. Some of the stones still sit where they were originally found. Others have been moved to adorn entrances to museums, hospitals, and schools. So what do experts know, and what remains rocky about this mystery?

THE CLUES

For decades, researchers have speculated about the origin and purpose of these great spheres. Here are some clues they've found to round out what we know:

SPHERES' YEARS By using radiocarbon dating on ancient pottery and other artifacts found near the stones, scientists estimate that the stones range in age from 500 to 1,000 years old.

SHAPING HISTORY Some spheres have marks where they appear to have been pecked, pounded, and smoothed.

ROUNDED UP Some of the spheres were discovered clustered together in patterns that may relate to the position of the sun, stars, or the moon.

CENTRAL AMERICAN BANANA PLANTATION

THE THEORIES

BASED ON THE AGES of nearby artifacts, like pieces of pottery, some anthropologists believe the oldest spheres were created between A.D. 600 and 1000 and that an early culture of people in the region continued to craft them until the 16th century. Those people left behind pottery and other ancient treasures in the same areas where the spheres have been found.

Some experts believe the ancient artisans who made the spheres probably used small stones as hammers to sculpt larger rocks into spheres. Dings and divots on the stones are the marks left behind from the process.

As for the purpose of the stones, anthropologists think they may have been placed in patterns as some kind of ancient calendar related to weather and the growing seasons. One archaeologist discovered that a pair of buried spheres line up with the rising sun on certain days. This could mean that the people who created the spheres were using them to track days. Others believe the stones were symbols of status: After all, it would have taken a lot of human power to craft, shape, and move them. Perhaps a high-ranking individual, or an important village, had the spheres made as a display of power and prestige.

STONE AND CLAY FIGURES FOUND NEAR THE SPHERES

Today, only a small percentage of the spheres are in their original locations, hidden in forests or resting on mountaintops. Others have been moved to parks, are used in cultural celebrations, or sit outside government buildings. One was even shipped to Washington, D.C., where it rests outside the Costa Rican embassy.

The annual Festival of the Stone Spheres commemorates the cultural significance of the stones.

THESE **TOWERING TOMBS** HAVE WITHSTOOD THE **TEST** OF **TIME.**

These colossal
CREATIONS
can be seen from OUTER SPACE.

THE BACKGROUND

THE PYRAMIDS OF EGYPT—burial tombs for kings and their treasures—have probably been dusted and debated more than any other ancient artifacts on the planet. These magnificent monuments have towered high above the Sahara in northern Egypt for about 4,000 years. They're the last of the ancient Seven Wonders of the World still standing. Centuries of curious visitors have stood on the desert sand and pondered the pyramids. But these ancient stone structures don't give up their secrets easily. Questions about the pyramids still stand as strong as the structures themselves, like who built these massive monuments and—since they didn't have modern machinery at the time they were constructed—how exactly did they do it?

The shape of Egypt's famous pyramids may have been inspired by the triangular shape of the sun's rays.

THE DETAILS

THE GREAT PYRAMID AT GIZA measures 754 feet (230 m) square and 479 feet (146 m) tall. It's the largest pyramid ever built. Constructing this massive structure might have taken 30 years and millions of limestone blocks, each weighing an average of 2.5 tons (2.3 t). It's part of a complex of pyramids in the desert that includes the Pyramid of Khafre, the smaller Pyramid of Menkaure, and the Great Sphinx.

THE CLUES
The questions surrounding these ancient pyramids still perplex scientists and Egyptologists today. How could humans transport, lift, and place these heavy blocks on an increasingly tall building without modern tools or even the wheel, which hadn't been invented yet? Here are a few clues we have to go on:

HOME SWEET HOME In 2002, researchers unearthed a vast complex of barracks—complete with ancient mud bed platforms and cooking areas—near the pyramids. They were filled with ancient artifacts, like shards of ancient pottery, trash, and bones from cows and other animals the inhabitants ate.

WORK FOR HIRE Excavations of a nearby cemetery revealed the oldest intact Egyptian sarcophagus, or coffin, ever found by modern archaeologists. It was discovered inside a tomb inscribed with the ancient Egyptian words for "overseer of the administrative district."

PROOF IN THE PAINTING An ancient Egyptian wall painting shows workers pulling a large statue on a wooden sledge. One worker in the image appears to be pouring water to wet the sand out in front.

DIAGRAM OF THE GREAT PYRAMID

a boat of Pharaoh Khufu, found in the Great Pyramid in 1954

THE THEORIES

THESE MAGNIFICENT monuments have mystified people for centuries. One Greek historian who visited the pyramids in 450 B.C. thought that it must have taken as many as 100,000 captive slaves to build them. But modern archaeologists now believe that it was more like 30,000 workers and that they were paid laborers, not slaves.

The 2002 discovery of the ancient barracks revealed where these workers would have eaten and slept when they weren't busy building. The village appears to have contained open-air courtyards and separate areas for baking and roasting, eating, and sleeping, as well as spaces for copper working and pottery making. Archaeologists think that this complex housed skilled workers who lived there year-round. Then, when the Nile flooded in the late summer and early autumn, farmers would have traveled from their fields to Giza to pitch in on building the pyramids.

Experts think the laborers were organized into teams, with each team having a boss or overseer. Animal remains found at the barracks show that these bosses—like the overseer unearthed from the nearby cemetery—likely ate prime meat like beef, while workers dined on sheep and goats.

The discovery of the barracks finally revealed who built the pyramids, but what about *how* they did it? In 2014, researchers from the University of Amsterdam published a study suggesting that ancient Egyptian workers could have used something like wooden sleds to haul tons of heavy stones and statues to a building site. In a laboratory, researchers re-created desert conditions, and then experimented with the best way to pull a heavy load over the sand. They found that when they wet the sand down, they reduced friction, enabling the sled to glide over the sand instead of plow through it. The team thinks that ancient Egyptian workers used this technique to make pulling their heavy loads possible—a theory backed up by the discovery of that ancient wall painting that appears to show a worker doing exactly that.

Despite these new discoveries and ideas, mysteries remain. How did ancient artisans stack the stones to keep them standing all these centuries? What lies inside the great structures? The chances of finding answers to all the questions might be stacked against us.

AN ARTIST'S SKETCH OF WORKERS BUILDING THE GREAT PYRAMID

EXTERIOR OF THE GREAT PYRAMID

BLOOD FALLS

BELIEVE IT OR NOT, THIS GORY WATERFALL IS *NOT* GUSHING BLOOD.

THE BACKGROUND

1 **SEEPING FROM** the snow-covered mountains of Antarctica's Taylor Glacier, a blood-red waterfall appears to pour 50 feet (15 m) down into frigid Lake Bonney. The falls are named for their color, but scientists have struggled for more than a hundred years to understand the heart of this mystery: Of course it's not blood that gives the water its vivid color ... but what is it? And with temperatures so far below the freezing mark, how can liquid flow at all?

THE DETAILS

2 **EXPLORERS FIRST DISCOVERED** the frozen waterfall in 1911. From a distance, it does look like blood

FALLS

is gushing out. But an up-close look reveals that the liquid is actually moving·very slowly, due to extremely cold temperatures that average around 1.5°F (-17°C). And despite what your eyes tell you, it's not really blood.

THE THEORIES

3 **EXPERTS SAY** it all started about two million years ago when the Taylor Glacier, part of Earth's East Antarctic Ice Sheet, moved over a group of very salty rivers and lakes, sealing them under 1,312 feet (400 m) of ice with no light or oxygen.

Thomas Taylor, the geologist who discovered the falls, hypothesized that red algae growing in the water as it seeps through the glacier might account for the water's strange color. Years later, in the 1960s, another geologist, Robert Black, theorized that the water-fall's color arises from the iron in the underlying bedrock, not from algae. He argued that when iron-rich water rises to the sur-face and meets oxygen, it turns red, giving the falls their freaky appearance. With no hard evidence to back up either side, the debate turned ice-cold.

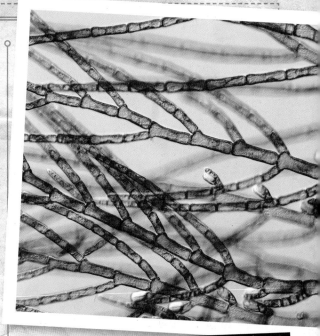

A SAMPLE OF RED ALGAE

NEW EVIDENCE REVEALED!

IN A STUDY PUBLISHED IN 2017, a team of scientists including National Geographic Emerging Explorer glaciol-ogist and geophysicist Erin Pettit traveled to Taylor Glacier to solve this bloodstained riddle once and for all. The team used radio echo sounding technology to map out a body of underground water under the glacier. They believe that when the glacier sealed the water beneath the ice sheet millions of years ago, ancient microbes were preserved along with it. The microbes digest iron particles, which turn the water red when they're pushed out into the air through fissures in the glacier. (The same thing happens when iron rusts.) If the researchers are right, that means the gory sight has been a long time in the making—the water takes I.5 million years to seep to the surface. So, has this frosty time capsule given up all its secrets—or is there more to this cold case?

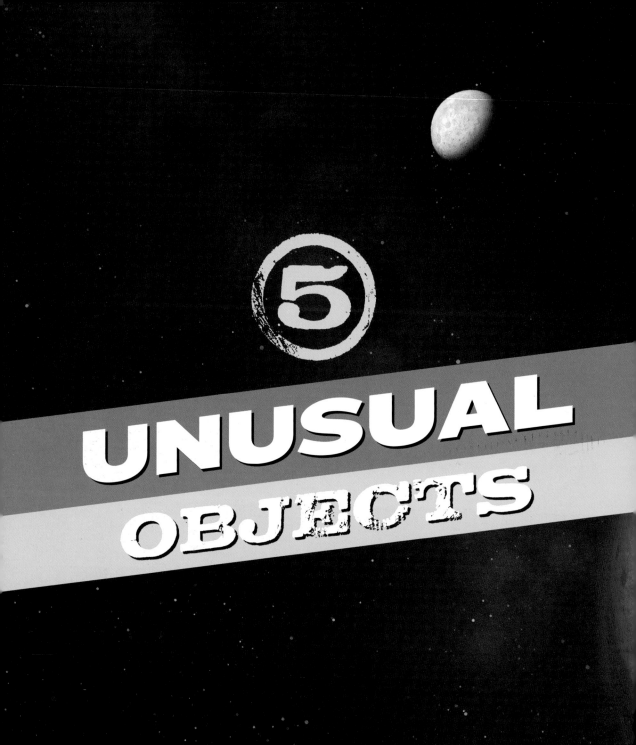

5

UNUSUAL
OBJECTS

HANG ON! Did you see that? By now, we know that the world is a mesmerizing, mystifying place, full of things still unexplained. But wait just a minute—it's about to get even weirder. From hidden planets to ancient batteries with surprising power sources to someone's shoes that were lost (and then found 2,000 years later), this chapter is full of bizarre discoveries that seem to defy explanation. Flip the page to figure out why scientists are still scratching their heads over these uncanny objects.

an artist's depiction of what Planet Nine might look like

Scientists have nicknamed this
MYSTERIOUS
and **GIGANTIC** globe
"George," "Jehoshaphat,"
and the "Planet of the Apes."

PLANET NINE

THIS PUZZLING POSSIBLE PLANET HAS GOT ASTRONOMERS PERPLEXED.

THE BACKGROUND

IF YOU THINK we have our solar system all figured out—think again! Consider its size: Mars is 33.9 million miles (54.6 million km) away—and it's our closest planetary neighbor! With so much space out there, there are still corners of our solar system that we have yet to explore—or even gaze at through a telescope. Is there anything lurking out there that we don't know about? Some astronomers think the answer is yes. They say there might be a mysterious, undiscovered planet hiding behind Neptune. They don't know much about it, other than it's gigantic—and that it's so far away that it takes up to 20,000 Earth years to orbit the sun. They call this mysterious object Planet Nine. But does it really exist?

THE DETAILS

HANGING OUT AT THE EDGE of the solar system, way beyond Neptune, is the Kuiper (KY-pur) belt. This icy ring is made of floating rocks, comet parts, and things too small to be considered planets, like Pluto (which astronomers classify as a dwarf planet). While observing the belt in 2014, astronomers Mike Brown and Konstantin Batygin saw something strange: The orbits of many smaller objects in the Kuiper belt had lined up, as if the gravity of some unseen object had a hold on them. But what could be pulling on all that space stuff? Experts spent more than a year investigating.

THE CLUES
Researchers have made their best guesses, or hypotheses, about what could be out there based on the evidence they've discovered. Here are a few clues about what they think they know about this potential planet:

➔ **GIANT-SIZE GRAVITY** Chunks of rock and ice in the Kuiper belt behave as if whatever is pulling on them is something big like a planet.

➔ **NEPTUNE-LIKE** The magnitude of its gravitational pull suggests that this mystery planet could be the size of Neptune, about 10 times bigger than Earth.

➔ **ICE GIANT** Research suggests the planet—if it exists—would be covered in ice and surrounded by a thick layer of gases.

NEPTUNE

Our solar system includes the sun, plus eight planets. Could there be one more?

007 TG422

2013 RF98

2004 VN112

2012 VP113

Sedna

2012 GB174

These six distant objects all line up in the same direction, tilting in the same way toward some unknown gravitational force that could be Planet Nine.

Planet Nine

DR. MIKE BROWN AND
DR. KONSTANTIN BATYGIN

THE THEORIES

ASTRONOMERS BROWN AND BATYGIN believe that Planet Nine is the real deal. They created a computer model to track the movement of the Kuiper belt objects. They plugged different scenarios into their program to try to figure out what was causing the objects' odd behavior and found that only one thing explained it: a distant—but massive—planet. Brown and Batygin think this giant planet has never been noticed before because it's so far away—about 10 times farther from the sun than Pluto. The search for this shy planet has been like an interplanetary game of hide-and-seek.

Brown and Batygin believe the hidden planet—if it really is that—might have formed closer to the sun and been blasted out into space when the solar system was very young. As for the planet's makeup, a squad of scientists in Switzerland used its estimated size, orbit, and distance from the sun to figure

out that it probably has a cold and icy surface but is likely hot and rocky at its core.

Many astronomers agree with Brown and Batygin. One was so sure of the planet's existence that he told the *New York Times* he'd bet $10,000 the planet is real. But other researchers doubt the existence of an extra planet hiding at the frosty fringe of the solar system. They say other objects similar to Planet Nine have been found, but none of them have turned out to be planets, casting doubt on this one. Thrilling fads about found planets, they say, have come and gone without enough evidence. The search to prove that the planet is real, or that the whole hypothesis is stardust, is a major case of TBD, or to be determined.

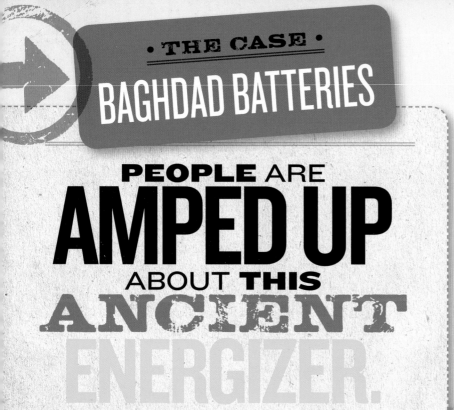

PEOPLE ARE AMPED UP ABOUT THIS ANCIENT ENERGIZER.

Experts have replicated these brain-bending **BATTERIES,** charging them up with ... **GRAPE JUICE!**

BAGHDAD, CIRCA 1917–1919

THE BACKGROUND

IT MIGHT SHOCK YOU to learn that humans could have harnessed electricity thousands of years before Benjamin Franklin ever experimented with his kite during a storm. In 1938, an archaeologist discovered a dozen or so 2,000-year-old jars that scientists believe may have provided power long before it was "invented" by Westerners. But the containers and how they were constructed have left experts scratching their heads. Could these uncommon artifacts indeed be ancient dead batteries? What powered them? And what in the world were these things used for?

TURKEY

SYRIA

IRAQ

IRAN

Baghdad

SAUDI ARABIA

KUWAIT

EUROPE

ASIA

IRAQ

AFRICA

THE DETAILS

THE CORRODED, five-inch (13-cm)-long clay jars were discovered during an archaeological dig in the 1930s near Baghdad, Iraq, by German archaeologist Wilhelm König. The site is near the area where ancient Mesopotamians would have lived. Each jar had an interior copper cylinder with one iron rod on the inside and one poking out of the top through a sealant of ancient asphalt.

THE CLUES

Scientists are working hard to flash some light on these ancient batteries. Here are a few clues that have helped energize their ideas:

- **RUSTY RELIC** The vessels showed signs of corrosion, probably caused from an acidic liquid, like vinegar or wine.

- **TO THE POINT** Some of the batteries were found with objects that appear to be needles.

- **CHARGED UP** Replicas of the batteries have produced voltages from 0.8 to nearly two volts of electricity.

THE THEORIES

EXACTLY HOW did these ancient batteries conduct themselves? No one can say for sure exactly what this ancient power source was powered by or why the technology went dark. Experts speculate that acidic liquids like vinegar or wine might have powered the Baghdad Batteries via electrically charged particles found in the liquids. Vinegar and wine both contain water and small amounts of acid. As they break down, positive and negative particles, or ions, form. The ions can carry an electric current through water. Replicas of the objects have been shown to produce a surprising amount of energy for something so old—four or five of these batteries would have been enough to power an iPhone. Some scientists believe the batteries may have been used in the process of gilding or electroplating, which was an ancient metal-plating technique in which electricity was used to transfer particles of metals like silver and gold to coat less valuable metals.

Some experts say the batteries' purpose may have had something to do with medical treatments. The ancient Greeks were known to have

LARGE SCALE ELECTROPLATING FACTORY

COPPER

SILVER

NICKEL

used the power of electric rays to numb a person's pain. Some people think the Baghdad batteries might have been used to amp up acupuncture treatments in which needles are inserted at specific points in the body to stimulate a nerve.

We may never discover whether these ancient artifacts were actually batteries or, if so, what they powered—but this is one charged-up mystery.

C

LEYDEN JARS, A WESTERN VERSION OF BAGHDAD BATTERY TECHNOLOGY

HIDDEN SHOES IN EGYPTIAN TEMPLE

THESE **ANCIENT** SHOES HAVE **KEPT** THEIR SECRETS ALL **LACED** UP.

THE BACKGROUND

IT'S NOT EASY to get around without your kicks. Throughout the millennia, shoes have protected people's feet as they walked countless miles. Styles and construction have changed with the times, from animal hides tied around the ankle to technologically advanced space boots that have walked on the moon. Shoes go where we go and can give clues to where the wearer has been. In 2004, Italian archaeologists working in Egypt had a mystery afoot when they discovered a jar filled with ancient shoes. It was hidden in a small space between two ancient brick walls of a 3,000-year-old Egyptian temple built for Pharaoh Amenhotep II. Finding a jar of ancient shoes is weird enough—but it gets weirder when you consider that most people in ancient Egypt wore sandals, a totally different type of shoe than the ones that were found. So who did they belong to and how did they end up tucked into a wall of this temple? So far, these tongues aren't wagging.

EUROPE ASIA
EGYPT
AFRICA

Mediterranean Sea

ISRAEL
JORDAN
SAUDI ARABIA
LIBYA
Nile R.
Red Sea
Luxor
E G Y P T
S U D A N

The oldest **SHOE** ever found dates back **5,500 YEARS!**

a burial chamber in the Temple of Amenhotep II near Luxor, Egypt

THE DETAILS

THE ANCIENT JAR contained seven slipper-like shoes, two pairs in children's sizes and the rest for adults. They would have been tied by tightening knots that passed through openings on the front of the shoe. The delicate, tasseled leather slippers were stuffed in that clay jar for centuries. It was found in an area known back then as Thebes, called Luxor today. It's a short walk from the banks of the gushing Nile River.

THE CLUES

The real history of these ancient shoes has, well, slipped through the cracks. But here are a few clues that tie up what we do know:

- **TIMEWORN TRACKS** Carbon dating has shown that the clay jar that held the shoes for all of these years is about 2,000 years old.

- **WATER SHOE** One of the adult shoes in the jar has a folded leather strip called a rand that was used to reinforce the stitching and keep mud and water out.

- **WEAR AND TEAR** One of the adult shoes gave a clue about its owner. It had a circular worn-out area common in shoes worn by people who have a bunion, or a deformed toe.

THE THEORIES

IN EGYPT'S UNFORGIVING and hot, dry desert climate—especially thousands of years ago, when the shoes were stashed—pretty much everyone wore sandals. Ancient footwear expert André Veldmeijer analyzed the shoes and found that they appear to have been designed not for the desert but for somewhere wetter. An extra leather strip would have reinforced the shoes' stitching for extra protection in muddy or rainy conditions. A rand found on the shoe was known to experts to be a device used to reinforce a shoe—but it was thought to have been used much later, in Europe's medieval period. That led Veldmeijer to believe that the shoes were probably constructed outside of Egypt. He also thinks that the quality and construction of the sandals meant they were expensive—probably a status symbol for the family who owned them.

original placement of shoes as discovered

THE ARCHAEOLOGY SITE WHERE THE SHOES WERE FOUND

Another theory gaining traction is that the shoes were worn by someone with sore feet. The leather on one shoe shows wear that indicates the person who wore the shoe may have suffered from a painful condition, commonly known as a bunion, in which the person's big toe grows inward toward the other toes. Another shoe showed signs of multiple repairs—a clue that it carried more weight than the other shoe in the pair. Could the person who wore the shoes have had an uncomfortable limp? It's likely. Otherwise, the wear on the shoes would have been more equal.

As to why the owners hid the shoes in the temple and never came back to retrieve the fancy footwear, the experts are still undecided. Veldmeijer says fighting or unrest in the area might have caused the owners to stash the shoes and run. But we'll never know for sure. The answers to this mystery may be tied up in knots for all eternity.

ACTUAL SHOES FOUND

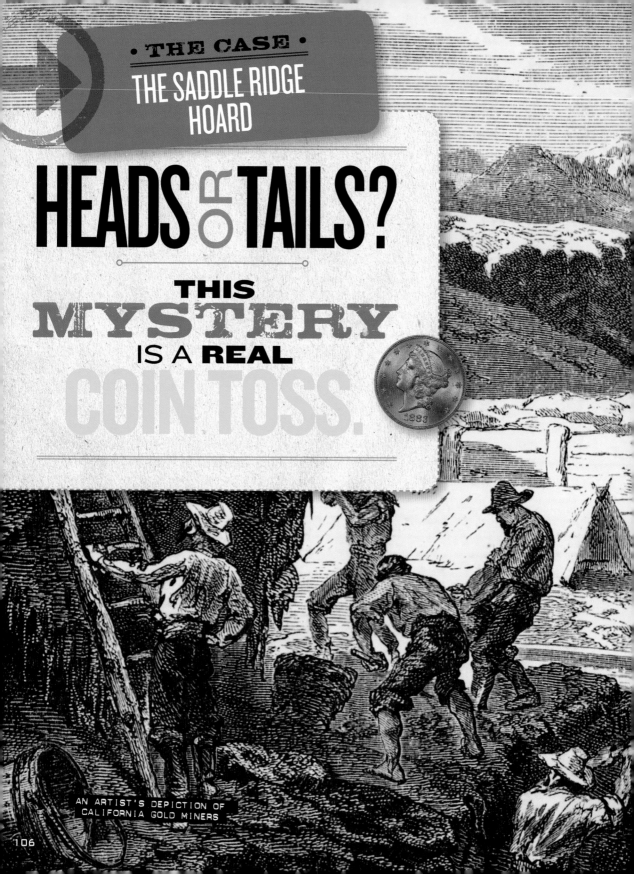

HEADS OR TAILS?

THIS MYSTERY IS A REAL COIN TOSS.

AN ARTIST'S DEPICTION OF CALIFORNIA GOLD MINERS

THE BACKGROUND

OREGON

CALIFORNIA

Gold Country

NEVADA

PACIFIC OCEAN

ARIZONA

YOU NEVER KNOW what might be hiding right under your nose! One lucky California couple hit the jackpot in 2013 when they noticed a rusty tin can sticking out of a hillside while walking their dog along the same trail they'd hiked for years. They dug it out, scraped the moss off of it, carried it home, and pried it open. Inside was a cache of old gold coins! The couple went back for more, and the loot turned out to be the largest stash of gold ever found in the United States. But the fantastic find has folks begging for an explanation: Who left all that gold behind? Why and when, and why didn't they come back for their buried treasure?

Most of the Saddle Ridge Hoard coins were **DOUBLE EAGLES,** or $20 gold pieces, one of which could be worth about **$1 MILLION** today.

THE DETAILS

IN TOTAL, the lucky couple found eight decaying cans full of coins, including 1,411 gold coins in mint condition, dated between 1847 and 1894. Most of the coins were made at the San Francisco Mint. At the time, it processed gold nuggets found by prospectors searching for gold. At face value, the coins were worth about $28,000. But in today's market value, the historic coins could be worth $10 million.

THE CLUES

Historians, gold-seekers, and anybody who likes a good treasure hunt have been dying for details about the Saddle Ridge Hoard since it was discovered. We don't know much about the who and the why, but here are some clues that help us add up this money mystery:

- **NEWS FLASH** An old newspaper clip from around 1900 reports that a suspiciously similar amount of coins had been stolen from the U.S. Mint.

- **OLD MONEY** The dates on the coins spanned almost 50 years.

- **GOLD RUSH** The location of the hidden coins is in California's Gold Country, site of the Gold Rush of 1849.

THE THEORIES

SOME COIN EXPERTS and historians speculate that the coins had been stolen and were hidden by an outlaw trying to stash his or her loot so he or she wouldn't be caught. Old newspapers report a theft from the San Francisco branch of the U.S. Mint in the early 1900s—for about the same amount of money later discovered in the Saddle Ridge Hoard.

On the other hand, some experts doubt the coins came from the mint because the dates

GOLD PROSPECTORS

on the coins span several decades. The mint would have produced and distributed coins as they were manufactured, as opposed to storing them.

Others say the hoard's original owner could have been a prospector who traded his mined gold for coins. Perhaps the prospector preferred to "deposit" his coins in the earth for safekeeping (unlike most people who, around this time, began keeping their money in banks). Today, many of the coveted coins have been sold to collectors. Will we ever know who buried the coins or why? Don't put your money on it.

THE LONG-LOST COINS AND THE RUSTY TIN THEY WERE DISCOVERED IN

U.S. MINT, SAN FRANCISCO, CALIFORNIA

THIS IMMORTAL MYSTERY MAY NEVER BE LAID TO REST!

THE BACKGROUND

1 **A SHROUD IS** a plain piece of fabric used to wrap a body before burial. But this ghostly shroud is no simple cloth. If what some experts say is true, this wisp of fabric has mysteriously survived for more than a thousand years and holds serious religious significance. Many believe the tattered, thin, 13-foot (4-m)-long cloth surrounded the body of Jesus Christ when he was buried, some-time around A.D. 30. But is this treasured religious relic—known as the Shroud of Turin—for real? Scientists have been trying to stitch together the pieces of this mystery for more than a century.

THE DETAILS

2 **THE BLOODSTAINED** Shroud of Turin is one of the most sacred treasures in the world— and one of the most debated. It appeared mysteriously in the mid-14th century in a church in France. No one could explain where it came from. Then, in 1898, an Italian photographer took a photo that added a new layer of strange to the shroud: The image appeared to highlight the blurry outline of a human body on the fabric. Scientists got busy investigating the photo in addition to the fabric itself. Some believe a negative of the photo (in which the dark parts are light and the light parts are dark) shows a suspicious bloody pattern. The wounds that would have left the pattern of bloody marks shown in the photo negative are consistent with those that Jesus Christ would have suffered at the time of his death in Jerusalem. Today, the mightily mysterious shroud is kept in northern Italy at Turin's Cathedral of Saint John the Baptist. But could this piece of linen really be the religious icon's burial garment?

THE THEORIES

3 **ONE GROUP** is convinced the image was simply painted on the shroud. Then, in 1902, a French anatomist who had studied the shroud declared the blood was real and not some painted-on fraud. But if the Shroud of Turin is the real thing, it would have to have stayed hidden for more than 13 centuries before mysteriously appearing at the church in France about 600 years ago.

In 1978, an international team of scientists got rare access to investigate the specimen. They brought seven tons (6.4 t) of equipment to Italy and worked 24 hours a day for five days. Their investigation found no sign of paint or ink that would have pointed to the shroud being a fake. They declared the shroud's image to have been left by the wounded man that it covered. But was that man Jesus Christ?

In 1988, experts used carbon dating technology to test the age of the shroud. They concluded that it was from between 1260 and 1390, more than 1,000 years after Jesus Christ had been alive. In 2005, another study claimed the relic was 3,000 years old. Both of these claims cast doubt on the idea that this

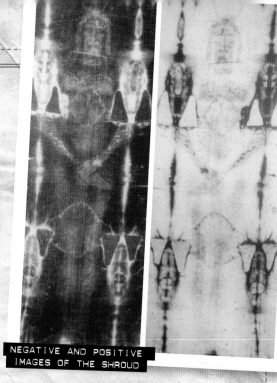

NEGATIVE AND POSITIVE IMAGES OF THE SHROUD

shroud was worn by Jesus Christ. But some believers still insist the shroud belonged to Jesus, saying the proof is a footprint on the shroud that contains traces of dirt and limestone consistent with Jerusalem during the time of his life. In the end, discussions, investigations, and theories about the famous shroud have led to nothing but spools of questions and tangled threads.

NEW EVIDENCE REVEALED!

IN 2013, scientists from the University of Padua retested what it believed to be bloodstained fibers from the 1988 investigation. Using high-tech analysis including infrared light, they dated the fiber to be from between 300 B.C. and A.D. 400, which was the time that Jesus Christ lived.

On Easter Sunday that year, Pope Francis I spoke about the shroud, but he didn't let on as to whether he believes that it held the body of Christ or not. One thing we do know: This topic is shrouded in years of mysteries that are not likely to be wrapped up anytime soon.

CURIOUS CURSES

These terra-cotta warriors were built to protect an emperor, but did they also carry a curse?

BEWARE ALL WHO PASS THIS PAGE: These next mysteries go beyond bad luck—they're cursed. From a car that dooms its passengers to death to a mummy that unleashes bad luck on anyone who dares enter his tomb, these bearers of misfortune would probably send most running for the hills. Some brave souls have ignored the risk and ended up paying the ultimate price. But could these stories be all exaggeration and hype? Or are they the real deal?

FEAST
YOUR EYES
ON THIS DIAMOND OF
DOOM.

In the early 1900s, the
HOPE DIAMOND
was referred to as the
"DIAMOND OF DISASTER."

THE BACKGROUND

WASHINGTON, D.C.
UNITED STATES

OHIO
PA.
W. VA.
MD.
KY.
Washington, D.C.
VIRGINIA
TENN.
NORTH CAROLINA

HAVE YOU EVER WONDERED how a diamond forms? Think back a billion years ago, and then imagine a bit of hardened carbon trapped 100 miles (161 km) below the Earth's surface. Ancient volcanic eruptions blasted bits of kimberlites—chunks of igneous rock that often contain the hardened carbon crystal we know as diamonds—closer to the surface of the Earth. After a few millennia of cooling, *voilà!* A diamond is born.

The famous Hope Diamond is a huge and dazzling rare blue stone celebrated for its size, color—and deadly history. It has been worn by royalty, glittered on the necks of wealthy socialites, and been stolen by jewel thieves. Legend has it that in the 1600s, a treasure hunter pried this super sparkler from the face of an ancient Hindu idol, or statue. His newfound good fortune turned into his downfall when he was eaten alive by wild animals. According to the legend, Hindu gods cursed the blue diamond forever to punish the thief.

Is the Hope Diamond—one of the world's most valuable, and notorious, jewels—the bearer of bad luck? Flip the page and decide whether you think this curse is rock solid or just a gem of a tale.

The history of the mysterious and beautiful Hope Diamond has been rocked by stories of intrigue, mystery, and a real gem of a curse.

THE DETAILS

AFTER IT WAS supposedly stolen by the ill-fated treasure seeker in India, the impressive diamond was sold to King Louis XIV of France in 1668. Back then the diamond was larger, cut into a heart shape, and called "The French Blue." The stone remained the property of French royalty for more than 100 years. But when revolution hit in the late 1700s, King Louis XVI and Queen Marie Antoinette—who had been accused of betraying France—fled for their lives. The French government confiscated the royal jewels but didn't protect them very well. The diamond and other precious gems were later stolen in a huge jewel heist in 1792. The French Blue was lost to history for a few decades, until 1812, when a suspiciously similar and stunning blue diamond—now with a different cut—appeared in the collection of a diamond merchant in London in 1839. The Hope family purchased it. Then American millionaire Evalyn McLean bought the diamond in 1911 for $180,000. After her death in 1947, a diamond merchant named Harry Winston bought McLean's jewelry collection. In 1958, he donated the 45.5-carat, walnut-size Hope Diamond—valued at more than $200 million—to the Smithsonian Institution where it has resided ever since.

THE CLUES

Over the course of the gem's colorful history, many of the Hope Diamond's owners have been struck with seriously bad luck. Some may say the curse is a crock ... but perhaps these bloodcurdling clues will convince you otherwise:

D FOR DISASTER After the diamond was stolen from the French royal family, King Louis XVI and his wife, Marie Antoinette, were beheaded. Many years later, after Lord Francis Hope came to possess the diamond, his wife left him and he had to sell the pricey stone to pay off massive debts.

SERIOUSLY SUSPICIOUS Wealthy socialite Evalyn McLean owned the Hope Diamond and thought the curse was hogwash. But in the years following her pricey purchase, two of her children died, her husband left her, and she fell into serious financial trouble.

RISKY DELIVERY In 1958, a mail carrier named James Todd delivered the diamond by registered U.S. mail to its present home: the Smithsonian Institution in Washington, D.C. Within a year Todd suffered two accidents—one crushed his leg and the other caused a head wound. Later, his wife died, his dog died, and his home was partially destroyed by fire.

PRESENTATION OF THE DIAMOND TO THE SMITHSONIAN

KING LOUIS XVI

MARIE ANTOINETTE

EVALYN MCLEAN WEARING
THE HOPE DIAMOND

THE THEORIES

CULTURAL ANTHROPOLOGIST Richard Kurin says there's little truth to the tale of the Hope Diamond's curse, and that all the sinister stories are just eerie coincidences or just plain untrue. For example, he says, there's no way the initial treasure hunter was eaten by wild animals after stealing the stone, because he had to have made it out of India alive in order to sell the jewel in France.

Kurin says it's the diamond's astonishing weight, clarity, and color that make it so famous. But many scholars believe the diamond's curse is actually its best feature and has heightened its extreme value. (The Smithsonian Institution says it's priceless, but the rock could be worth as much as $250 million.) Throughout its history, some of the diamond's owners are known to have exaggerated the tales of the diamond's cruel history, increasing its rabid reputation—and its price—when the stone was up for sale.

The Smithsonian Institution claims the curse is pure legend. Today, you can see the Hope Diamond on display at the Smithsonian's Museum of Natural History, where the big, blue glittering gemstone is the Smithsonian's most visited exhibit. But don't look for too long ... you never know if the curse is contagious!

117

8,000 CLAY WARRIORS— each one with a different face— still guard the emperor's **TOMB.**

THE GREAT WALL OF CHINA

TERRA-COTTA WARRIORS

THIS EMPEROR WENT **ALL OUT** FOR THE AFTERWORLD.

EMPEROR QIN SHI HUANG

THE BACKGROUND

CHINA'S FIRST EMPEROR, Qin Shi Huang, who ruled 2,200 years ago, wanted to make sure he was well remembered—and well protected—after he died. First, he built the massive Great Wall of China that spans more than 5,500 miles (8,851 km) to leave his mark. Then, he started building his tomb. For thousands of years after the emperor died in 210 B.C., few knew where he was buried. But in 1974, farmers digging a well discovered a life-size fired clay (or terra-cotta) soldier buried underground near the old Chinese capital of Xianyang near the city of Xi'an. Then they found another and another and ... well, you get the picture. These mysterious clay commandos have left archaeologists and historians with a lot of questions: Who built them for the emperor? How did they do it? And is it possible that the ancient king armed his clay warriors with the power to curse anyone who disturbed them?

ASIA
CHINA

RUSSIA
MONGOLIA
CHINA
Xi'an
INDIA

THE DETAILS

DURING QIN SHI HUANG'S TIME, emperors planned their burials as soon as they started ruling. To build his epic work of afterworldly art, the emperor would have ordered as many as 700,000 workers (many of them likely slaves) to labor night and day to sculpt the thousands of soldiers—complete with weapons, horses, and individualized faces—from clay. Legend says the statuesque fighters wielded a fierce curse. Nobody has carved out exactly what about the story is fact and what might be a tall tale.

THE CLUES Researchers have chiseled, dug, and dusted to get close to these soldiers, who still protect secrets from the past. Here are a few things the investigations have revealed about their mysterious origins:

FAR FROM HOME DNA analysis of skeletal remains in mass graves near the tomb complex indicates that at least one worker was from Europe. Bronze figures of ducks, swans, and cranes found outside the tomb suggest influence from Greek artists.

TO ARMS! Chinese archaeologists found that the clay soldiers were armed with real weapons, including bronze swords, bows, and about 40,000 arrowheads, which were bundled to fit in a quiver (a pouch that holds arrows for a bow).

COINCIDENCE OR CURSE? The farmers who dug up the first soldier suffered a rash of bad luck after the discovery. A newspaper story published at the time reported that the Chinese government seized the farmers' village. After that, some of the farmers contracted diseases and died early deaths.

CAVALRYMAN WITH HORSE

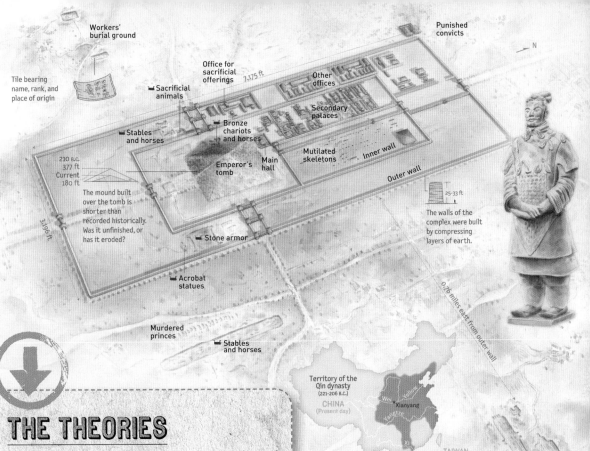

Workers' burial ground

Punished convicts

N

Tile bearing name, rank, and place of origin

Office for sacrificial offerings 7,175 ft

Other offices

Sacrificial animals

Secondary palaces

Bronze chariots and horses

Stables and horses

Mutilated skeletons

Inner wall

210 B.C. 377 ft Current 180 ft

Emperor's tomb

Main hall

Outer wall

3,196 ft

The mound built over the tomb is shorter than recorded historically. Was it unfinished, or has it eroded?

25-33 ft

The walls of the complex were built by compressing layers of earth.

Stone armor

Acrobat statues

0.76 miles east from outer wall

Murdered princes

Stables and horses

Territory of the Qin dynasty (221-206 B.C.)

CHINA (Present day)

Wei Yellow

Xianyang

Yangtze

TAIWAN

MAP OF COMPLEX

THE THEORIES

THEORIES ABOUT who built the clay soldiers for the emperor and how they did it stretch around the globe. Scientists using remote-sensing, ground-penetrating radar and core sampling have revealed the emperor's tomb complex to be much larger than once believed—almost 38 square miles (72.5 sq km). To complete such a big project, the emperor may have had to bring in workers from outside China. Experts have unearthed skeletal remains of people believed to be workers who were likely from Europe—as well as artifacts bearing traits from their homelands.

As for why Qin Shi Huang created the stone statues in the first place, most theories point to a single reason: to protect himself after he died, which was typical for emperors of his time. Each soldier was outfitted with a weapon, and Shi Huang kept his burial location hidden so he could stay safe in the afterlife. Legend has it that Shi Huang's son ordered all the artists working on

the project buried alive in mass graves after the job was finished so they couldn't tell anyone anything about his father's location. Could that terrible treachery have been enough to start a dreadful curse?

But some believe the emperor bestowed a curse that was waiting to unleash bad luck on anyone who discovered his soldiers. Plenty of spooky occurrences—even death—did indeed occur after the site was uncovered. To this day, no one has opened the tomb itself where the emperor is said to have been laid to rest thousands of years ago, guarded by his clay warriors. Curse or no curse, many of this mystery's secrets remain cemented in scary silence.

KRUGER MILLIONS

NOBODY KNOWS **WHERE** THESE MYSTERIOUS MILLIONS **MIGHT** HAVE BEEN MOVED.

THE BACKGROUND

WHEN PAUL KRUGER, president of the South African Republic from 1883 to 1900, had to flee his palace, he likely had a few things to check off his list: Grab treasured family heirlooms? Maybe. Important papers? Probably. Stash his loot? Definitely. In the late 1800s near the end of the Anglo-Boer War, Kruger led a resistance against British rule. Legend says he issued orders that if the enemy attacked the capital city of Pretoria, the reserves of the national bank—which included millions of dollars' worth of gold and silver bars, coins, and diamonds—should be divided up and hauled into the veld, or grassland, to be hidden. We know that Kruger was forced to flee Pretoria when the British invaded the city in 1900. But to this day, no one knows what happened to the money. Could it still be buried? Or was it *ever* buried to begin with?

AFRICA
SOUTH AFRICA

NAMIBIA
BOTSWANA
SWAZILAND
Johannesburg
LESOTHO
SOUTH AFRICA
ATLANTIC OCEAN
INDIAN OCEAN

PAUL KRUGER

This hoard of **GOLD** could be worth **$30 MILLION** today.

Pretoria, South Africa, 1890s

THE DETAILS

KRUGER, the South African Republic's first president, died in exile without revealing what happened to the loot. Most of his supporters also perished in the war, leaving no one to say if the republic's great fortune—which included valuable one-ounce gold coins featuring President Kruger's profile—had been stashed, and if so, where its hiding spot was. Many treasure-seekers have searched for the missing millions over the years, but so far they've turned up empty-handed.

THE CLUES

Nobody knows where Kruger's people hid the South African Republic's money—if they hid it at all—but time has turned up a few clues:

MISSING MONEY In 1900, when the British assumed control of the South African Republic, 1.5 million pounds (680,000 kg) in gold coins and bars was missing from the bank.

X MARKS THE SPOT A 1949 map (drawn by the man who was in charge of the South African mint at the time the gold went missing) appeared to hint at where the treasure is buried.

GOLDEN COINS In 2001, newspaper reports said Zulu workers in a remote South African town called Ermelo had unearthed a cache of gold Kruger coins. According to the reporting newspaper, details about the location were kept quiet out of respect for the many people who lost their lives during the war.

PRESIDENT KRUGER, CENTER

PRETORIA MINT, 1900

THE THEORIES

MANY TREASURE-SEEKERS theorize that when Kruger found out war was coming, he wanted to make sure the money didn't end up in enemy hands. As troops got closer to the capital, Kruger and his supporters may have loaded the treasure on a train and hightailed it out of there to the safety of neutral Switzerland. When the next president arrived to take over, the bank's vaults tallied up short. Some suspect that Kruger secretly used the money to help his side win the war.

But what if not all of the Kruger millions made it out of the country? After Kruger made his escape, stories swirled about odd packages being unloaded from his train in the dead of night. Could Kruger have buried some of the money along his escape route for safekeeping, where it's hidden to this day? Treasure-seekers certainly would like to think so. But no leads—including the 1949 map—have led to any treasure.

In 2001, a newspaper reported that Kruger coins had been unearthed on a farm. According to the paper, the missing millions had been divided in three parts when war broke out. One part was loaded onto wagons and carried to the town of Ermelo, where it was spotted and attacked by patrolling British soldiers. Kruger's supporters were able to hide the wagons, probably by burying them. But they were later killed, and the treasure's location was lost, until the farm workers dug them up. But the find was never confirmed—leading many to say this paper's "story" was more fiction than fact.

Some say there's still a mother lode waiting to be found in South Africa's lush, lion-filled terrain. But nobody—not even the best bounty hunters—has been able to find proof. Or if they have, they're keeping the treasure all to themselves.

SWAMP IN KRUGER PARK

KING TUT'S TOMB

DID THIS **BOY KING'S** TOMB SEAL UP A WICKED CURSE?

THE BACKGROUND

ONLY 10 YEARS OLD when he came to power, the boy king Tutankhamun is one of the most famous pharaohs of ancient Egypt. That's because when archaeologists discovered his tomb back in the 1920s, they found much more than a gravesite. King Tut was mummified and laid to rest with a glittering treasure trove that had been hidden under debris for thousands of years. But opening up the 3,000-year-old relic may have been a risky choice. Egypt's "mummy curse" is said to threaten death to anyone who disturbs resting royalty buried in the Valley of the Kings. Did the scientist who opened Tut's golden tomb unleash a wicked jinx leading to death and destruction? Turn the page and let's see what you think of this mummified mystery.

EUROPE ASIA
EGYPT AFRICA

Mediterranean Sea
ISRAEL
JORDAN
LIBYA
Valley of the Kings
SAUDI ARABIA
Nile R.
Red Sea
E G Y P T
S U D A N

Archaeologists have re-created King Tut's tomb to learn more about the famous pharaoh.

Ancient Egyptians MUMMIFIED not only their people, but also their pets: cats, birds, and even CROCODILES.

THE DETAILS

AFTER YEARS OF SEARCHING for lost pharaoh tombs, British archaeologist Howard Carter and his sponsor, Lord Carnarvon, practically stumbled upon steps that led down to a burial chamber hidden beneath a pile of rubble, not far from the tomb of Ramses VI, another famous pharaoh. Soon they were peering into a pristine four-room chamber that hadn't been entered since King Tut's death. It took Carter the next 17 years to study the thousands of objects found inside. The glitzy tomb contained toys, jewelry, gold statues, and perfume. Newspapers heralded the discovery and printed photographs of the glittering solid-gold coffin and the magnificent mummy it contained. But Lord Carnarvon didn't celebrate for long. Eight weeks after the big discovery, he was dead after suffering from an infected mosquito bite. Others who came close to the tomb would suffer, too, like Egyptologist Zahi Hawass, who studied the mummy up close in 2005. That is, he did until his work was delayed, first because of a death in the family, then again because of a massive storm. When Hawass finally got the mummy into his lab, his scanning machine broke. Could the curse be real?

THE CLUES
Tombs can be fun for archaeologists, but most living people prefer a little more fresh air, especially when there might be a wicked curse circulating. Here are a few clues that may explain what's up with this troubling "curse":

- **MOLDY OLDIE** Two dangerous species of mold—*Aspergillus niger* and *Aspergillus flavus*—are known to live in ancient tombs.

- **GOING BATTY** Bats often make their home in excavated tombs. Their droppings carry a fungus that can cause disease.

- **WICKED WORDS** Inscriptions on ancient Egyptian tombs made hostile threats saying that anyone coming near the tombs would be eaten by lions, snapped in two by crocodiles, or bitten by scorpions and snakes.

HOWARD CARTER EXAMINES A MUMMY.

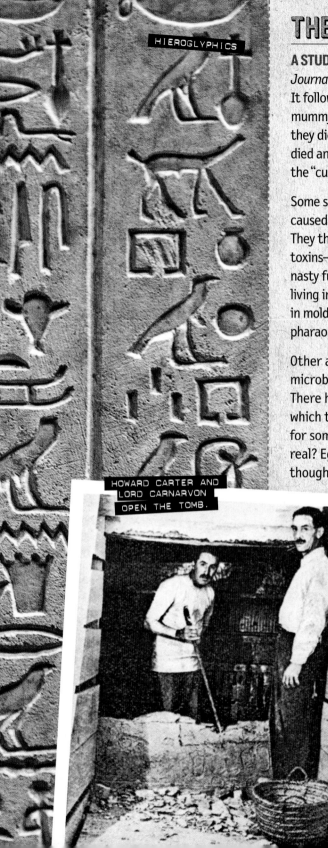
HIEROGLYPHICS

HOWARD CARTER AND LORD CARNARVON OPEN THE TOMB.

THE THEORIES

A STUDY PUBLISHED by the *British Medical Journal* in 2002 says this curse is all tall tale. It followed 44 people who had been near the mummy in the early 1920s and tracked when they died. The data didn't show that any of them died an early death, despite their connection to the "curse."

Some say Carnarvon's death might have been caused by real-life germs, not a mystical mummy. They think the tomb may have contained harmful toxins—either deadly mold living on the walls, nasty fungus carried in the droppings of bats living in the cave, or ancient bacteria growing in moldy 3,000-year-old food left to feed the pharaoh in the afterlife.

Other archaeologists doubt the story that microbes from inside the tomb killed anyone. There has never been a documented case in which tomb molds or bacteria were responsible for someone's death. So, could the curse be real? Egyptologist Salima Ikram says that though it's unlikely King Tut's mummy put a hex on archaeologists, the idea of a cursed tomb did originate in ancient Egypt. She says ancient walls were inscribed with "curses" meant to scare people away—like an ancient alarm system designed to protect the dead. Whether the curse had to do with mold, deadly spells, or dangerous animals, heed its warning and steer clear of Tut's tomb.

THE CURSE OF THE BILLY GOAT

A BAA-D DAY
FOR THE CUBS!

THE BACKGROUND

1 **THE CHICAGO CUBS** were once one of the most popular and successful major league baseball teams in America. Between 1876 and 1945, the team won the National League Pennant 16 times and played in the World Series (which began in 1903) 10 times, winning in 1907 and 1908.

But the glory came to a screeching halt on October 6, 1945, just after the end of the Second World War. It was during game four of the World Series that year. Before the game got underway, the stadium had refused entry to a four-legged fan—a goat named Murphy. The animal's owner is said to have put a hex on the team for denying him his good-luck charm. He left the stadium, yelling, "The Cubs ain't gonna win no more!" And he wasn't kidding. The Cubs lost big that day to the Detroit Tigers. Was it because of what would become known as the Curse of the Billy Goat? For decades, many have believed the startling curse to be true.

THE DETAILS

2 **A FAN** and the owner of the local Billy Goat Tavern in Chicago, William "Billy Goat" Sianis, had two tickets to that World Series game—one for himself and the other for Murphy, who he believed would bring luck to his favorite team. When Sianis complained to the owner of the Cubs after an usher turned the goat away, the Cubs owner said the goat wasn't welcome "because the goat stinks." After the team lost that day, Sianis sent a letter to the Cubs owner asking, "Who stinks now?" And for the next 71 years, the Cubs had a serious losing

(left) the Chicago Cubs in 1945

streak. They didn't win any pennants or make it to the World Series. Instead they became known as the "lovable losers." Believers say the losses don't lie and that the Cubs were seriously cursed by the goat. But are they right? Or just kidding around?

(above) Sam Sianis, nephew of William, took his goat to opening day in 1984 to try to break the curse. It didn't work.

THE THEORIES

3 **SPORTS FANS CAN BE SUPERSTITIOUS,** and many die-hard Cubs fans say everything and anything can play into the outcome of a game: the weather, wearing a lucky hat, or the obsessive rituals of the players, like the particular way a batter adjusts a glove, digs a cleat into the dirt, or taps the bat on home plate. If any of those things goes wrong, all might be lost. Many Cubs fans believe the Curse of the Billy Goat is the only thing that can explain the Cubs' long losing streak.

But some experts say people invent explanations like curses to turn something bad, like a bad loss (or years and years of losses) into something good, like nostalgia for the good old days when the Cubs seemed to always win big. Perhaps having something thrilling and mysterious to talk about, like the Curse of the Billy Goat, helped distract from the heartache of losing. Over the years, trying to make sense of the curse became a thrilling game of its own, passed down through generations of Cubs fans.

NEW EVIDENCE REVEALED!

IN ONE of the biggest wins in baseball history, on October 22, 2016—after going 71 years without winning a pennant—the Chicago Cubs broke the losing streak that fans had long blamed on the Curse of the Billy Goat. On that day in Chicago, Illinois, U.S.A., the Cubs beat the Los Angeles Dodgers 5–0. The win sent the Cubs to the 112th World Series, which they won, too.

What's weird is that Billy Sianis, the goat-owner said to have uttered the original curse, died 46 years earlier on October 22. So was it just a superstition all along? Or did the curse finally run its course?

7

UNNATURAL NATURE

MOTHER NATURE has an unlimited supply of surprises up her sleeve. Biologists, geologists, and other -ologists spend their lives studying Earth and its mysteries, trying to better understand the beautiful puzzle of the natural world. We might think we have it all figured out, but then we discover something that is far-out, wild, or seems to defy any natural explanation. Take, for example, a cartoonlike, colorful spotted lake that looks like a fanciful illustration. Or a supersize sea monster that snacked on whales 150 million years ago. Or an area in the Caribbean that seems to have an appetite for the planes and ships passing through. Are these things for real? Sometimes the natural world is stranger than fiction.

Lightning strikes a plane down in the Bermuda Triangle.

Despite artists' illustrations and computer-generated models based on scientists' observations of fossils, we actually know very little about what the big marine reptile really looked like.

PREDATOR X

THIS MASSIVE MESOZOIC MYSTERY WILL LEAVE YOU SPEECHLESS.

Svalbard
—NORWAY
EUROPE
AFRICA

ARCTIC OCEAN
Svalbard

ATLANTIC OCEAN
NORWAY

THE BACKGROUND

GO DIGGING UP SECRETS from the past and you never know what buried giants you might find. In June 2008, a Norwegian paleontologist working on the barren Arctic island of Svalbard made a find of epic proportions: the nearly complete fossil of what turned out to be a massive, monstrous, short-necked and toothy new pliosaur, a type of big extinct marine mammal with paddle-like limbs. The reptile would have lived 150 million years ago—at the same time as dinosaurs. But like any great mystery of history, this freaky Jurassic find came with a lot of questions. What exactly was this prehistoric sea monster, what did it look like, and just how dangerous was it?

THE DETAILS

WHEN THE FOSSIL was first discovered, this massive, big-headed aquatic hunter, later nicknamed "Predator X," made headlines around the world as the most daunting hunter of all time. It breathed air, had huge flippers, and sported a stubby but heavy-duty tail. Its head alone stretched nearly 10 feet (3 m) long—about the length of a car. Its entire body measured about 50 feet (15 meters) from gnashing teeth to thrashing tail, and it weighed about 50 tons (45 t). This funky fossil got its own species name to reflect its identity: *Pliosaurus funkei,* or *P. funkei* for short. So what else do we know about this mysterious megamonster?

THE CLUES
Scientists are still searching for details that will give us the whole story on this fascinating ocean behemoth. One thing we know for sure: It had a heck of a bite. These clues can help flesh out a more complete picture:

- **TERRIBLE TEETH** Predator X had teeth the size of cucumbers (only sharp) and a bite that likely would have out-chomped a *Tyrannosaurus rex.*

- **ARMED AND DANGEROUS** Analysis shows that stealthy Predator X had longer flippers than other pliosaurs.

- **SPECIALLY ADAPTED SNIFFER** The ancient creature had special internal nostrils adapted to smell prey underwater.

AN ARTIST'S RENDERING OF PREDATOR X

LEFT: showing a size comparison; BELOW: making plaster casts at the excavation site

THE THEORIES

ACCORDING TO JØRN HURUM, whose team found the specimen, Predator X is the most powerful marine reptile ever discovered. Its alligator-like snout was filled with huge, sharp teeth, and fossils show that it was larger than a full-grown orca—likely twice the size of other ocean predators from the Jurassic period. Based on the size of its teeth and powerful bite, it likely chomped on massive prehistoric fish and other marine reptiles like plesiosaurs and ichthyosaurs.

Based on its anatomy and its powerful, over-size paddles, experts think Predator X likely deployed a deadly sneak-attack method. It could have circled in the depths undetected, sniffing out prey through huge aquatic nostrils. Then, it would have surged upward to attack without warning, grabbing its victim in its massive maw, shaking it, and ripping it apart. One of the ancient beast's favorite snacks was likely *Kimmerosaurus*, a smaller long-necked plesiosaur.

Other experts agree that Predator X was terrifying but doubt that the fearsome hunter was as big as the original estimates. Guesstimating the size of creatures that lived millions of years ago from puzzle pieces of bone fragments and fossils is not an exact science, after all. We may never get to know this heavy-duty character as much as we'd like to ... but, on the other hand, maybe what we already know is terrifying enough.

MYSTERIES HIDE IN THE DEPTHS OF THESE PUZZLING PUDDLES.

This strangely spotted body of water can be found near the Okanagan Valley in the desert of British Columbia, Canada.

CANADA
BRITISH COLUMBIA

YUKON TERRITORY

CANADA
U.S.

PACIFIC OCEAN

ALBERTA

BRITISH COLUMBIA

Spotted Lake

CANADA
U.S.

THE BACKGROUND

THIS POLKA-DOTTED LAKE in British Columbia, Canada, looks like a watercolor set with puddles of blue, yellow, and green paint. In the springtime, the water that bubbles up to form this mysterious geochemical wonder is diluted and murky brown. But by summer, most of the water has evaporated, leaving the colorful puddles that Spotted Lake is named for. Some spots stretch 50 feet (15 m) across. To add to the beauty of this kaleidoscopic conundrum, each puddle is ringed by sparkling crystals. Smaller, newer rings appear and sometimes overlap. What causes this mysterious and magical lake to sprout these colorful spots each year?

THE DETAILS

MANY PEOPLE in western Canada believe Spotted Lake is sacred. It's known by the Okanagan people as Kliluk and thought to be the grandfather of other lakes in the region. They also believe that the lake's mud has healing powers. Some people—and their children—even bathe in the rings to take advantage of its protective powers.

THE CLUES

Geologists and cultural archaeologists have studied the mysterious site for years. Here are a few clues that help us understand the rocky mystery that lies beneath the surface of this very special place:

HOLD THE SALT No fish swim in the lake's waters, which contain toxic levels of salty minerals like magnesium sulfate, calcium sulfate, sodium sulfate, and trace amounts of silver and titanium.

MAGICAL MUD For centuries, Aboriginal people in the area have used mud from this lake to heal wounds and treat aches and pains.

PERFECT TEMP The groundwater doesn't bubble up because it's boiling. Instead, pressure from underground pushes it up and out.

BEAR

CARIBOU

THE THEORIES

GEOLOGISTS SAY this spring-fed lake bubbled up about 10,000 years ago when a stranded glacier melted and created a depression in the earth. When snow melts in the spring, the water collects underground. That groundwater travels through fractures and faults in the area's underlying bedrock.

Geologist Murray Roed believes the key to this colorful mystery lies within the valley's ancient bedrock. It has a strangely high concentration of minerals that are absorbed by the groundwater as it flows through the bedrock. When the water is pushed up onto the surface of the earth, the 38-acre (15-ha) lake fills and bubbles like a pot of mineral-rich stew, creating these mysterious and colorful spots.

But the minerals don't just color the water: They also make it highly toxic if ingested. The deer, caribou, moose, bears, coyotes, cougars, bighorn sheep, and hundreds of species of birds that live in the Okanagan Valley around Spotted Lake stay clear of the lake. What other wonders is Spotted Lake hiding? We may never know.

MOOSE

SINK YOUR TOOTH INTO THIS UNDERWATER ENIGMA!

Narwhals sometimes scrape their tusks against one another. It looks like they are fencing, but scientists think they are just identifying each other.

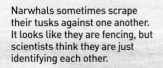

SPIRAL NARWHAL TUSK

THE BACKGROUND

NARWHALS ARE ONE of the world's hardest-to-find creatures. That's because they spend so much time deep under water, often below the ice in their Arctic environment. These marine mammals can live to be 90 years old and grow to about 3,500 pounds (1,587 kg). Like many whale species—including relatives such as bottlenose dolphins, belugas, harbor porpoises, and orcas—narwhals live and travel in groups of two to 10 individuals, called pods. Experts have classified them as "near-threatened," which means narwhals may be on a path to becoming an endangered species. About 80,000 of them are left in the wild. But elusive narwhals have a mysterious attribute that makes them unlike any other whale: a single spearlike tusk that grows out of their head. This mystery has scientists scratching their own heads. What's the purpose of these terrific tusks that look like a supersize unicorn's horn?

where unicorns of the sea live

ASIA
EUROPE
PACIFIC OCEAN
ARCTIC OCEAN
ATLANTIC OCEAN
NORTH AMERICA

THE DETAILS

ONCE HARVESTED and sold as unicorn horns for 10 times their weight in gold, a narwhal's tusk is actually a tooth that pokes through the animal's upper lip when it's about three months old. This is the only tooth the whale develops. Over time, the tusk can grow to be about 10 feet (3 m) long—about half the length of the whale's body and as long as a regulation NBA basketball hoop is tall! As long as humans have been able to observe these beautiful creatures, there's been debate about what exactly the narwhal's terrific tusk is used for. So what do experts know?

THE CLUES

Are they for decoration, attracting potential mates, fending off predators, or something else? Scientists don't have all the answers yet. These whales are shy and elusive, which makes them very hard to study. Here are some clues experts have found to help solve these gnawing questions:

- **SUPER SENSITIVE** Narwhal tusks are made of ivory. But inside, they are filled with thousands of sensitive nerves that could provide the animals with information about the environment around them.

- **TUSK FOR ONE** Usually, only male narwhals grow tusks.

- **EYE SPY** Video footage recorded in 2017 shows narwhals whacking Arctic cod with their tusks before eating them.

MAN WITH A NARWHAL TUSK

MALE PEACOCK

MALE LION

Male narwhals swim in Lancaster Sound off Baffin Island in Canada.

THE THEORIES

OVER THE YEARS, scientists have spouted many different theories about how a narwhal uses its tusk. From ice-breaking tools to sound detectors, they've speculated about seemingly every possibility. In 2014, a group of researchers (the group included marine biologists, zoologists, and even dentists!) deduced that the tooth might be used to gauge the temperature and saltiness of the sea, like an antennae. The team thought this ability might be an evolved trait to help the animals avoid areas of ocean water that might freeze over and trap them.

But other marine biologists disagree. If the tusks served as a survival adaptation to help the narwhal live successfully in its environment, they believe both males and females would grow tusks. But female narwhals don't usually grow a tusk (although a few have been known to grow them), and yet they thrive in their Arctic home. These scientists think it's more likely that the male's tusk is used to attract females, like a male peacock's flashy feathers or a male lion's luxurious mane.

In early 2017, theories about the purpose of the tusk shifted after researchers in remote northeastern regions of Canada witnessed some never before seen narwhal behavior. The whales appeared to chase after fish and then smack the prey with their tusks, stunning them. Experts think the behavior is a hunting tactic that makes the fish easier for the narwhals to catch and eat. For many scientists, this new finding has knocked out any remaining questions about the tusk's purpose. But the most important mystery still remains: how to protect these mythical, marvelous—and very rare—animals.

BERMUDA TRIANGLE

THIS PETRIFYING POLYGON HAS AN APPETITE FOR **BOATS** AND **PLANES.**

The Bermuda Triangle has long been the subject of curiosity and speculation. Over the years there have been many disappearances that the public has deemed suspicious. So what's really going on?

VIOLENT blasts of gas from under the seafloor are sometimes called **"BURPS OF DEATH."**

THE BACKGROUND

THE BERMUDA TRIANGLE is a huge area of the Atlantic Ocean bounded roughly by Miami, Bermuda, and Puerto Rico. Alarming reports about unexplained disappearances and weird instrument readings in the area started stacking up in 1945 when five Navy planes took off from their base in south Florida on a routine training mission. As they flew over the area known as the Bermuda Triangle, they reported compass problems ... and then were never seen again. Search parties combed the sea but didn't turn up the people or their planes. After that, stories of ships and planes lost in the Bermuda Triangle starting popping up with more and more frequency. No one knows for sure what the deal is with the morbidly mystifying Bermuda Triangle. But if you're ever there, buckle up— you might be in for a bumpy ride!

UNITED STATES

ATLANTIC OCEAN

Gulf of Mexico

Bermuda Triangle

Caribbean Sea

THE DETAILS

EVIDENCE OF THIS watery mystery started pouring in around the mid-20th century, but unusual occurrences in the Bermuda Triangle date back even further. Christopher Columbus recorded bizarre compass readings while sailing through the area in 1492. The tricky triangle is home to some of the deepest underwater trenches in the world—between 19,000 feet (5,791 m) and 27,500 feet (8,229 m) below sea level. Nobody knows for sure what dangers lurk below.

THE CLUES
Scientists, oceanographers, and meteorologists have tried to dredge up more evidence to unlock the mystery. So far, the triangle's holding its secrets underwater, though we do have a few clues about this deep blue mystery:

 VANISHING ACT As many as 300 planes and boats have disappeared in the Bermuda Triangle during the 20th century.

STORM CENTRAL Most tropical storms and hurricanes in the Atlantic Ocean region pass through the Bermuda Triangle.

 BLAST OFF Massive craters on the seafloor in the area of the Bermuda Triangle may have been formed by exploding natural gas.

THE THEORIES

MANY THEORIES about the Bermuda Triangle have claimed to explain what happened to the missing boats and planes and their occupants. They cover everything from alien abductions to death rays from the lost continent of Atlantis, which some say sank there thousands of years ago.

Most scientists believe in more rational, documentable causes, such as the deadly spikes of volcanic rocks that dot the area and could easily spear a ship. Or the fact that the triangle-shaped area is extra-prone to stormy weather, with the kind of high waves and shifting winds that can swallow up a crew. Others argue that there's nothing strange going on here—it's just a matter of heavy traffic. One of the most heavily traveled shipping lanes in the world crosses through the Bermuda Triangle. The high number of ships and planes that pass through every day simply increases the likelihood of accidents.

In 2016, researchers at the Arctic University of Norway discovered giant craters—up to a half mile (0.8 km) wide and 150 feet (45 m) deep—off the coast of Norway. Scientists think these craters are formed by huge, explosive releases of gas that bubble up from deep inside Earth. Similar craters have been spotted at the bottom of the seafloor in the Bermuda Triangle, leading experts to theorize that the gas explosions creating the craters could also be causing violent turbulence in the water and in the air, which could explain all of those sunken ships and fallen planes. This mystery has surged on for years and years. And even after so much investigation, scientists can't agree on what causes all the ruckus in this terrible triangle of doom.

In 1945, a group of five U.S. Navy torpedo bombers vanished in the Bermuda Triangle. Then, the plane sent to find and rescue them also disappeared.

SIBERIAN SINKHOLES

WHAT'S CAUSING THESE CRAZY CRATERS IN NORTHERN RUSSIA?

THE BACKGROUND

1 **IF YOU'VE EVER WONDERED** what the inside of the Earth looks like, you might want to check out these astonishing sinkholes that are like portals into the center of the planet. When the massive and mysterious holes suddenly appeared in Siberia in 2014, scientists threw on their climbing gear and rappelled in to explore one of the terrifying and terrifically large hollows. Some of the craters measure more than 100 feet (30 m) across and have muddy, icy water at the bottom. So what caused these creepy craters to form, how many are there, and will more explode out of the Earth's innards anytime soon?

THE DETAILS

2 **AT LEAST SEVEN CRATERS** have since been detected by satellites, including one large hole that is surrounded by as many as 20 smaller craters. They all appear to have been blown open from the inside out, spewing rocks and dirt into the Siberian wilderness. And that's not all. Locals report hearing ominous

YAMAL PENINSULA
CRATER IN RUSSIA

noises, like booms and thuds, coming from within the craters, leading them to wonder if they're really just geological wonders... or portals to the underworld. Many of the Siberian sinkholes were discovered in northern Siberia's Yamal Peninsula, a name that means "end of the world" in the local language.

THE THEORIES

3 AFTER THESE DEPRESSIONS made headlines, possible causes started swirling. Everything from meteorites to stray missiles were offered up as explanations. Carolyn Ruppel, a scientist with the U.S. Geological Survey's Gas Hydrates Project, says satellite mapping suggests the holes actually have to do with "pingos," or plugs of ice that form near the surface of the Earth over time. When a pingo melts rapidly—as many have been recently, thanks to unseasonably warm temperatures in Siberia—it can cause areas of the Earth's surface to collapse, forming craters. Other scientists say the craters were formed by underground gas explosions. So what's forming these giant craters?

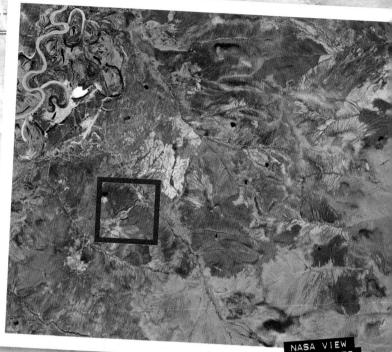

NASA VIEW OF THE SITE

NEW EVIDENCE REVEALED!

IN 2017, a new study revealed that these suspicious sinkholes are expanding. The Batagiaka crater in eastern Siberia, for instance, was already the largest of its kind, but it has recently widened to be more than a half-mile (0.8 km) long and almost 300 feet (91 m) deep. Scientists expect the craters to grow even wider (thanks to climate change and a warming of the Earth's thick permafrost) at a rate of about 30 feet (9 m) per year. Permafrost, made up of soil, rocks, and water, is a frozen layer of earth just under its surface. Now that you've got a "hole" lot of facts to ponder, what do you make of this pit-iful situation?

INTERVIEW

DIGGING TO SOLVE MYSTERIES

WITH
JØRN HURUM

JØRN HURUM

SINCE HE WAS A KID, Jørn Hurum has been following his curiosity and digging up answers to questions related to mysteries from millions of years ago. As early as when he was six years old, he dug up fossils outside his home in Norway. He wanted to know where the curious bones and rocks came from and what they meant. Today as a paleontologist, science educator, and National Geographic Explorer, he studies 150-million-year-old fossils found in Norway's Svalbard archipelago, north of the Arctic Circle. Hurum's got plenty to say about what we can learn from exploring history's mysteries and asking questions that don't always have easy answers. Here, he shares some of what he's learned:

IN SEARCH OF STORIES. When I was about six years old, I realized fossils were not just rocks, but could tell the history of life on this planet. I imagined fossils saying, "I am not a rock. I am a fossil. I have a story to tell." I collected fossils and created a museum in my room. All the visitors who came to our home had to be escorted through and have a proper showing of the exhibits. I wanted to learn everything I could about fossils because I thought they were so interesting.

PASSION PROJECT. Discoveries are exciting, when we find something new. It's like one of those scratch-off lottery tickets every time we dig. Sometimes we start digging and we might just find part of a skull or other bone. Sometimes, we find the skull and vertebrae—then you know it's a jackpot! Other things are exciting too, like flying in helicopters to remote digs. Or being on an Arctic island during a summer snowstorm and watching out for polar bears on the hunt.

PREHISTORIC PUZZLE. I have found fossils all over the world—like in the United States, Mongolia, Argentina, China, Canada, Kyrgyzstan, and Australia—and have studied dinosaurs, mammals, and marine reptiles. In Svalbard—that's the fossil-rich Arctic island where we do most of our research—our team mostly finds evidence of prehistoric marine reptiles, such as ichthyosaurs and plesiosaurs. One of the plesiosaurs we found is nicknamed "Predator X." (You can read more about this prehistoric and mysterious sea monster on page 134). Predator X was a fairly complete fossil: a flipper, a rib cage, and the back of a skull. But sometimes we find what I call "explodasaurus." That's when we find a skeleton spread over a large area due to weathering over time. We may find some ribs, vertebrae, or a skull in thousands of pieces. We then have to identify the entire animal from individual pieces. We have so far collected 60 skeletons of several unknown species of marine reptiles in this remote locality.

LOOKING BACK. The past has everything to teach us. Everything has a story. An old bone or an ancient artifact can help us understand how we evolved. To me, these treasures are witnesses to the past.

(Top) Jørn's team at the dig site in Norway

(Left) Jørn and team with part of Predator X's fossil

AFTERWORD

WHETHER IT'S an ancient arrowhead turned up by a growing tree in the forest, a funny-looking tarnished coin found buried in a rusty tin can, or a dusty prehistoric bone, artifacts and clues all around us (even those we haven't found yet) tell stories about our past. Reading about the past can offer clues to our future as humans. What can we learn from lost civilizations about human survival? What do lost treasures say about our history? What are the stars in the sky trying to tell us about our universe? Following your curiosity can almost become a superpower. If you're paying attention to the world around you and asking lots of questions, something you learn or discover might change the world one day or teach us all something about our world (and all of its mysteries) that we didn't know.

CAVE ART IN
ÇATALHÖYÜK

155

INDEX

Boldface indicates illustrations. If illustrations are included within a page span, the entire span is **boldface.**

INDEX

INDEX

ILLUSTRATION CREDITS

CREDITS

For curious young readers everywhere. –K.J.

Published by National Geographic Partners, LLC. All rights reserved. Reproduction of the whole or any part of the contents without written permission from the publisher is prohibited.

Since 1888, the National Geographic Society has funded more than 12,000 research, exploration, and preservation projects around the world. The Society receives funds from National Geographic Partners, LLC, funded in part by your purchase. A portion of the proceeds from this book supports this vital work. To learn more, visit natgeo.com/info.

NATIONAL GEOGRAPHIC and Yellow Border Design are trademarks of the National Geographic Society, used under license.

For more information, visit nationalgeographic.com, call 1-800-647-5463, or write to the following address:

National Geographic Partners
1145 17th Street N.W.
Washington, D.C. 20036-4688 U.S.A.

Visit us online at nationalgeographic.com/books

For librarians and teachers: ngchildrensbooks.org

More for kids from National Geographic: natgeokids.com

For information about special discounts for bulk purchases, please contact National Geographic Books Special Sales: specialsales@natgeo.com

For rights or permissions inquiries, please contact National Geographic Books Subsidiary Rights: bookrights@natgeo.com

Designed by Jim Hiscott

The publisher would like to thank the team who helped make this book possible: Ariane Szu-Tu, lead project manager and editor; Kathryn Robbins, art director; Sarah J. Mock, senior photo editor; Molly Reid, production editor; and Gus Tello and Anne LeongSon, design production assistants.

Trade paperback ISBN: 978-1-4263-3164-0
Reinforced library binding ISBN: 978-1-4263-3165-7

Printed in Malaysia
18/IVM/1